# A Traveler's Guide to Asian Culture

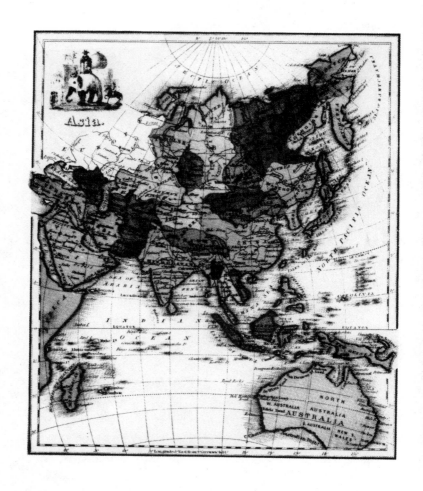

# A Traveler's Guide to Asian Culture

## Kevin Chambers

John Muir Publications
Santa Fe, New Mexico

For Joe and Lynda Silva

I wish to thank the following people for their assistance in this project: Mildred Chambers, Sim Chambers, Wesley Palmer. A special debt of gratitude is owed to my father, Byrl Chambers, who passed away during the preparation of this book.

John Muir Publications, P.O. Box 613, Santa Fe, NM 87504

First edition. First printing

Library of Congress Cataloging-in-Publication Data

Chambers, Kevin.
    A traveler's guide to Asian culture / Keven Chambers. — 1st ed.
      p   cm.
    ISBN 0-945465-14-9
    1. Asia—Description and travel—1951- —Guide-books.   2. Asia—
    Civilization.   I. Title.
    DS4.C43  1989
    950—dc20                                                    88-43528
                                                                      CIP

Typeface: Sabon and Bauer Bodoni Bold Condensed
Designer: Marcy Heller
Printer: Banta Company
Typesetter: Copygraphics


Distributed to the book trade by:
W.W. Norton & Company, Inc.
New York, New York

# Contents

## Etcetera

## Index

# Introduction

## Why Asia?

Asia has more than 5,000 years of history, more languages than there are varieties of sushi, and more culture than you can absorb in just one visit. The sheer magnitude of Asian history, culture, and art is enough to send even the most intellectually curious traveler in search of a new destination—preferably one with a bite-sized past.

But Asian culture is too much fun to pass up and too important to ignore. The intellectually curious traveler will find Asia to be an unrivaled adventure whether or not he or she knows the difference between a stupa and a torii. This book will tell you not only that you should walk clockwise around stupas and under torii but also *why* you should. If you are the kind of traveler I think you are, knowing why will enhance your adventure severalfold.

Because seeing and feeling history is more enlightening and less painful than reading a textbook, I have selected important pieces of Asia that will make history tangible to the traveler. You will not find Yoshikazu-san, the fifteenth-century Japanese shogun, in this book. He may have been important to his contemporaries, but he did not leave much behind for the twentieth-century tourist to see. If the effect of a historical person or event is not seeable, doable, or otherwise sense-able, it is not emphasized in this book.

Art reflects the conditions under which it is created. Religion has played a vital role in Asian culture, and most pre-twentieth-century Asian art reflects that religious vitality. Trying to understand this art without understanding the major religions of Asia is like trying to play mah-jongg[1] without reading the instructions. The most important aspects of Hinduism, Buddhism, and Islam are explained in the "Traveling Tools" section of this book—before we touch on much else. The proper mindset is a prerequisite for any enjoyable trip. The "Traveling Tools" section will help you get into the mood. As you begin to read, think of yourself as a Chinese calligrapher, rhythmically grinding the ink stick into liquid ink. Before beginning to write, his eyes focus on the blankness of the paper, his mind on the image he intends to create. When the moment comes, the characters take form with amazing rapidity and sureness of hand. We must be as properly prepared as the calligrapher—and as charged as his ink-soaked brush—before hitting the canvas of Asia. Otherwise, we cannot expect to create an experience of lasting quality.

## Yes, Virginia, Asia *Is* Part of the World

The next time you are browsing in the fine bookstore where you acquired this guide, thumb through some of the thick tomes with the words "world history" in their title. Chances are, Napoleon, Maria Teresa, and Karl Marx all warrant a page or two—perhaps even Pope Martin V gets a mention. But does Qin Shihuangdi, the creator of the Chinese Empire, get his name in the book? Nooooooooooo! Even Siddhartha Gautama, founder of the world's most popular religion (Buddhism), rarely merits a passing remark.

---

1. A complex Chinese board game in which players slap and shuffle tiles around the table with the utmost vigor and racket (often played during the wee hours of the morning in Chinese hotel rooms with paper-thin walls).

This blind spot in our historical rearview mirror has led many Westerners to believe that Europe has always dominated the world. In fact, Europe's dominance has been established only in the last five centuries. Sixteen-hundred years ago, the invading Huns of Asia were on the outskirts of Vienna, and the fate of Europe hung in the balance. Europe did not gain the upper hand until the Renaissance set the stage for modern science and machines. Many of us mistakenly speak of "Asia" or "the Orient," as if it shared a common culture in the same way that Europe does. The nations and cultures of Asia may have influenced one another in many ways, but they are also substantially different from one another. India and China share little in the way of historical experience or cultural attitudes. Practically, however, that large chunk of earth to the east of Europe must be called *something*, and historical usage has assigned it the name "Asia." As long as we remember that the unifying name does not imply a region of overriding common characteristics, there is no harm done.

## Your User's Manual

This guide is carefully organized to make the complexity of the Asian world understandable. "Traveling Tools" gives you the background you will need to make sense of almost everything you see in Asia— information about Asian religions to help you understand the art; explanations of architecture to help you see the path, frozen in carved stone and shaped wood, of Buddhism's migration across Asia.

"History and Culture" gives the fundamentals of Asian history through the ancient, classical, colonial, and modernizing periods. What sets this section apart from the average textbook are the "Sites" notes, which tell you where to see evidence of the episodes of history discussed in this book. If you are as spatially oriented as most humans, you will also appreciate the timelines at the end of the "History and Culture" chapters, which will give you a feeling for the chronological order of events and their relationships.

History is happening right now in Asia. Travelers and adventurers of today have as much opportunity as the Marco Polos of the past to

discover a new world for themselves. The "Exploring Modern Asia" section will show the way. "Before You Leave" includes recommendations for predeparture reading and tips for preparing for your adventure.

## Finding the Way

*A Traveler's Guide* gives you the historical, cultural, and artistic highlights of Asia and tells you where to find them. I do not tell you which bus to take to these sites or how to get back—that would simply duplicate the many fine guidebooks currently available. Pick up a good guidebook for each country you plan to visit—before you get there. Reading the guidebook and visualizing the trip beforehand will make the destinations easier to find and help you avoid wasting valuable time once you arrive.

## M.A.S.H. Geography

In an episode of "M.A.S.H.," the TV sitcom about a mobile medical unit in the Korean War, the actors repeatedly referred to Korea as being in Southeast Asia. In 1988, no less a venerable publication than the *Asian Wall Street Journal Weekly* repeatedly illustrated articles about Pakistan with a map that showed the Arabian Sea entirely covering Pakistan's neighbor, Iran. Even an American ambassador assigned to an Asian post during the Carter administration professed surprise when informed that Korea was a divided nation. So take heart—you are already much further along than Hollywood or the U.S. diplomatic corps.

The word "Asia" is derived from the Greek word for sunrise. Any Greek going to Asia would have to travel toward the sunrise to get there. Geographers consider Asia to be every bit of land east of the Ural Mountains and the Suez Canal. Those geographers more interested in cultural boundaries often exclude the Middle East and the Soviet Union from their definition of Asia. For the purposes of this book, I have excluded Soviet Asia and the Middle East.

"Southeast Asia" is a term that has developed in this century to include all the nations lodged between China, India, and Australia. The Philippines, Indonesia, Brunei, Singapore, Malaysia, Vietnam, Laos, Kampuchea (Cambodia), Thailand, and Burma are included in this grouping.

"Northeast Asia," also a recently popularized term, includes Japan and Korea. The far northeast portion of China (what was once Manchuria) is sometimes included in this group. "East Asia" generally refers to China (including Taiwan) as well as the Northeast Asian and Southeast Asian nations. "Far East," although a more ambiguous term, is usually synonymous with "East Asia." "South Asia" and the "Indian subcontinent" are used to denote the area south of the Himalayas—Pakistan, India, Bangladesh, Afghanistan, Nepal, Bhutan, and Sri Lanka.

The "Orient" is what Europeans used to call the area east of the Mediterranean Sea, which we now call the "Middle East." The word is derived from the Latin word "oriens" (east). The term gradually became applied to Asia as a whole and especially to East Asia. The "Orient" is less of a geographical term than a term denoting characteristics or qualities peculiar to the East.

"Indochina" encompasses Vietnam, Kampuchea, and Laos. France colonized and administered this region as a unit in the nineteenth and twentieth centuries. The region acquired this name due to its mixed Indian (Indo) and Chinese cultural heritage.

## Where Did Ceylon Go?

Many nations in Asia changed their names after gaining independence or changing governments. Others, such as Formosa (Taiwan) and the Chinese city of Canton (Guangzhou), never knew themselves by the names outsiders called them. The Chinese have known "Canton" as "Guangzhou" for a very long time—only in recent years did the West adopt the original Chinese name (despite our willingness to convert, the Chinese continue to call New York "Niu Yue").

The following is a list of place-names used by Westerners. In some cases the names are the same ones used by indigenous peoples—in

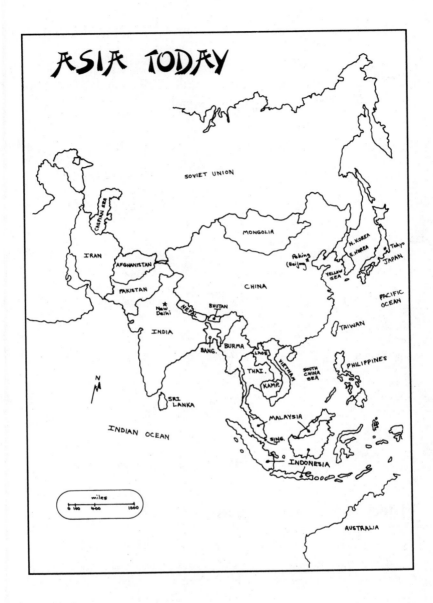

# ASIA TODAY

SOVIET UNION

CASPIAN SEA

IRAN

AFGHANISTAN

PAKISTAN

MONGOLIA

CHINA

Peking (Beijing)

N. KOREA

S. KOREA

YELLOW SEA

Tokyo

JAPAN

PACIFIC OCEAN

New Delhi

NEPAL

BHUTAN

INDIA

BANG.

BURMA

LAOS

THAI.

VIETNAM

KAMP.

TAIWAN

SOUTH CHINA SEA

PHILIPPINES

SRI LANKA

N

INDIAN OCEAN

MALAYSIA

SING.

INDONESIA

miles

0   100        400           1000

AUSTRALIA

other cases not. For instance, cartographers switched from "Chosun" to "Korea" in the early part of the twentieth century, but the South Koreans do not call their country "Korea"—they know it as "Hanguk."

| Old Name | New Name | Country |
|---|---|---|
| Batavia | Jakarta (Djakarta) | Indonesia |
| Benares | Varanasi | India |
| British Borneo | Sarawak and Sabah | Malaysia |
| Cambodia | Kampuchea | Kampuchea |
| Canton | Guangzhou | China |
| Ceylon | Sri Lanka | Sri Lanka |
| Chosun | Korea | Korea |
| Dairen | Luta | China |
| Dutch East Indies | Indonesia | Indonesia |
| East Pakistan | Bangladesh | Bangladesh |
| Edo | Tokyo | Japan |
| Formosa | Taiwan | Taiwan |
| Peking | Beijing | China |
| Port Arthur | Lushun | China |
| Quelpaert Island | Cheju Island | Korea |
| Siam | Thailand | Thailand |
| Yamato | Japan (Nippon) | Japan |
| Yezo (Jesso) | Hokkaido | Japan |

French Indochina became Vietnam, Kampuchea, and Laos.

## History Today, Gone Tomorrow

Many of the finest creations of man still survive in Asia—huge rock-hewn Buddhas, man-made caves filled with murals and carved reliefs, 4,000-year-old bronzes that rival anything made today. But what has not survived is heartbreaking. Much of India's greatest monumental art was allowed to fall into decay or to be broken up and used in new construction. The Chinese have melted down many of the ancient bronzes and pillaged their own temples—much of the destruction being committed as recently as the Cultural Revolution of the 1960s.

Whether you are looking at a Sung dynasty silk painting in a museum or at cave murals in India, realize that these objects probably have survived only by chance. In many cases, they are there for you to see only because humans forgot about them for a long time. Enjoy them, respect them, and do your part to help preserve them for those who come along after you.

# Western Authors on Asia

The late nineteenth and early twentieth centuries were exciting times to travel in Asia. The few Western generalist writers who traveled in the region during this period offer travelers of today a look at an Asia that will never be again. Reading their books before taking off for Asia will give travelers a valuable perspective.

Even those writers who traveled most widely in Asia tended to devote their keenest observations to the expatriate European community. This is quite understandable—virtually none of the Western writers could speak or understand the languages of the countries in which they traveled.

## Joseph Conrad

A quiet young Pole who hung around European expatriates in 1880s Asia, Conrad (born Korzeniowski) first came to Asia as a sailor on a coal ship that caught fire off the coast of Sumatra. Conrad puttered about the seas of Indonesia in 1887 and 1888 aboard the Vidar and experienced Malay villages and Dutch colonial officials, later recording them in his novels.

Conrad's tales of the East revolve around European exiles and expatriates—seamen, merchants, officials, and wanderers. Although Conrad deplored colonialism, the Asians appearing on the periphery of his stories are stereotyped as either noble savages or cunning primitives. Conrad's observations and brilliant storytelling nonetheless provide a look at Asia through nineteenth-century European eyes. Among Conrad's novels set in Asia are *Almayer's Folly, An Outcast of the Islands, Lord Jim, Typhoon,* and *The Nigger of the Narcissus.*

## George Orwell

An Englishman best known for his novels *1984* and *Animal Farm,* Orwell (real name Eric Blair) spent five years in Burma as a member of the Indian Imperial Police. He was born in the Bengal region of India in 1903 of expatriate parents. Orwell recorded his feelings about his sojourn in Burma in his first published novel, *Burmese Days.* His distaste for the kind of colonial imperialism he experienced in Burma is evident in this and subsequent works. A theme of oppression of the weak and poor runs through his life's works.

## Rudyard Kipling

Born in India in 1865 and packed off to England for education between the ages of three and seventeen, Kipling returned to Lahore (present-day Pakistan) in 1882 to write for a daily newspaper.

Kipling married an American and moved to Vermont in 1892, where he wrote *Jungle Book* while surrounded by snow. Kipling's early works dealt with Victorian India. Works of interest to the traveler in Asia: *The Man Who Would Be King*, *Departmental Ditties*, *Plain Tales from the Hills*, and *Kim.*

# Sites—Kipling

*Shimla, India*—This town in the Himchal Pradesh area of India was the scene of the stories in Kipling's *Plain Tales from the Hills.* This beautiful town on the side of a cool mountain was the seat of British colonial administration during the hot Indian summers. The most memorable way to arrive in Shimla is by rail from Kalka (near Chandigarh).

*Kyaikthanlan Pagoda at Moulmein, Burma*—Kipling immortalized this beautiful pagoda in his works.

## Somerset Maugham

One of England's best novelists and short-story writers of the early twentieth century, Maugham also traveled widely in Asia and wrote of his experiences. Maugham lavished most of his attention on the European expatriate circles in which he circulated. His books are peopled by diplomatic officials, merchants, missionaries, and seamen. *The Gentleman in the Parlour* (1930) was a travel book subtitled, *A Record of a Journey from Rangoon to Haiphong.*

Maugham traveled in China twice between 1919 and 1921 and painted a sharp but fictionalized portrait of China in his book *On a Chinese Screen* (1922). This book, since reprinted by Oxford University Press, is full of rich observations on the life and attitudes of the expatriate community circa 1920. On his second trip to China, Maugham also visited Indochina (Vietnam) and Malaya (Malaysia).

Maugham's experiences in Asia provided fodder for two of his plays, *The Letter* (made into a movie starring Bette Davis in 1940) and *East of Suez.* His realistic accounts of expatriate life in Asia often angered his former hosts, and Maugham was sued several times; his book *The Painted Veil* was recalled to appease the Acting Colonial Secretary of Hong Kong.

## Other Authors

*Isabella Bird Bishop*—An adventurous Englishwoman and travel writer who roamed widely in Asia at a time when it was almost unheard-of for a woman to travel alone. To avoid scrutiny, she wore men's clothing. *Korea and Her Neighbors* is an account of her travels in Korea, Manchuria (China), and Siberia in the 1890s. Her other travel books—*Unbeaten Tracks in Japan, Among the Tibetans, The Yangtze Valley and Beyond,* and *Chinese Pictures*—offer keen observations of nineteenth-century life in Asia.

*Pearl S. Buck*—A prolific writer of novels about China, such as *The Good Earth* and *Imperial Woman.* Her novel about Korea, *The Living Reed,* is set in the period from 1880 to World War II, when Korea was emerging from centuries of isolation.

*Shway Yoe*—His real name was Sir James G. Scott, an English civil servant in Burma for thirty years—much longer than George Orwell's stay in the country. His book *The Burman, His Life and Notions,* about Burman culture was originally printed in 1882 but has been reprinted in paperback.

# Travel Is (Not Necessarily) Broadening

Many say that travel is broadening. I do not believe so; I know too many frequent travelers who are just as narrow after 50,000 miles as they were before. Broadening the mind requires a concerted effort to do so. Proximity to a learning opportunity does not in itself guarantee anything. It is quite possible to see a thousand Buddhist temples without understanding any more about Buddhism than the person who never left home.

To take advantage of the opportunities presented by travel, we have to force our brains to react to new stimuli and to ask questions about why things are the way they are. Hurrying through a Jain temple, we may come to think that the massive statues of the Jain tirthankara saints seem simple and unimpressive. If we start to wonder why Jain artisans did not invest their images with the same vitality that their contemporary Buddhist counterparts did, we may learn that the Jain artisans' purpose was not to create an elaborate work of art but to represent the spiritual tirthankaras as personifications just human enough for the faithful to be able to identify with. Too much detail, too much personality would erroneously connote mortality to an impersonal Absolute. Without asking the question and learning the artisans' purpose, we would sadly miss a profound point.

# I.

# The Traveler's Tools

# 1

# Understanding Asian Art

On my first visit to the National Palace Museum in Taipei, I came away feeling, strangely enough, impressed but bored. I knew that I had seen some great works of art, but I did not understand what I had seen, nor did I appreciate its significance. And what we do not understand, bores us.

The numerous Shang dynasty bronzes and Sung dynasty landscape paintings were nice enough but I honestly felt that "once you've seen one, you've seen 'em all." Only later, when I read about the t'ao-t'ieh masks worked into the bronzes and compared them to later, less-skilled works, did I realize how unique those bronzes are.

When you head for a new destination, check out a book from the library and read about the place and its art before you get there. When you arrive, head for the best museum, look at all the objects on display and pick out a few that you like. After touring the country, return to the museum and look things over again at a slower pace; read all the explanations. When you get back home, reread the reference books while waiting on your film to be developed—this will help lock that new information into long-term memory. If you follow this procedure, you will not only understand more (and therefore appreciate more), you also will have more fun.

Many great Asian works of art currently reside in American and European museums. During the period of Western colonialism, many treasures of Asian art were taken back to Europe by the colonizers. In the twentieth century, American money brought many of the best works to American museums. To prepare for your Asian trip visit the Smithsonian Institution's Freer Gallery of Art in Washington, D.C., or the Los Angeles County Museum of Art, or the Nelson Gallery of Art in Kansas City. I have heard a lot of tourists say, "All these Buddhas look alike!" Standing before the 1,001 statues of the bodhisattva Kannon at the Sanjusangendo Temple in Kyoto, one is tempted to agree. You wonder: why didn't the artisans express their individual styles when they carved these wooden images? Try to remember: these artisans were not after creativity or self-expression; their objective was to copy as closely as possible existing classical images. Through faithful rendition, the powers of the original religious images could be transferred to new images. Almost like a magical potion—if the formula was not faithfully followed, the spell would not work.

## Messages in the Buddha's Ears

When viewing Asian art, look for distortions—variations from realism. Where there is a distortion, there usually is a message. The Buddha's ears often are portrayed abnormally long to remind the faithful that before he attained enlightenment, he was a prince, a member of a rich family that could afford heavy jewelry—jewelry that could pull the wearer's ears toward earth. The accurate representation of reality is generally less important in Asian art than in the West. In Asia, symbolism and mood take on greater importance. The painters of China, Korea, and Japan make a special effort to transfer their spirit (or the spirit of the moment) to the painting. Before the painter begins, he creates the proper mood by making careful preparations. The ink stick is slowly ground on the grinding stone until the ink and water attain the perfect consistency. The quasi-sacramental grinding motions have a calming, almost hypnotic effect.

To appreciate a painting—or any work of art—take the same slow, reverent approach that the artist takes in his preparations. Look for the spirit behind the canvas: what was the painter's mood when he executed this work?

Understanding how something is made adds to your appreciation of it. The Chinese did not invent the potter's wheel, but their late start did not prevent them from becoming the most accomplished potters in the world. They were able to excel by using high-temperature firing technology of bronze casting in pottery production. Knowing this helps one to see the connection between Shang bronzes and early stoneware.

Chinese painting is heavily influenced by the way the Chinese write their language. Chinese characters were (and often still are) written using a fiber brush and black ink. Both calligraphy and painting rely upon the Four Treasures: a brush, ink stick, ink stone, and paper.

Although brushes have been found in 2,300-year-old Chinese tombs, painting did not become popular until the Han dynasty (206 B.C.-A.D. 8). Rather than use liquid ink, the Chinese developed ink sticks of soot and glue that could last for years. The artist or calligrapher who wanted to brandish his brush simply ground the ink stick on the ink stone in a little water. Most ink stones are slabs of slate with a carved depression for the ink. Before long, these painting tools became art objects. Fine brushes are treasured. Ink sticks often are molded into designs.

## Artists to Look for

*Giuseppe Castiglione*—At the National Palace Museum in Taipei, you may encounter some Chinese paintings that look strangely un-Chinese. Chances are, you have found the work of Lang Shi-ning, better known as Giuseppe Castiglione. A Jesuit missionary who came to Macao in 1715, Giuseppe applied his considerable artistic talents to creating a hybrid European-Chinese form of painting. Look for his "Portrait of Hsiang Fei" or the "Fish and Water Grasses"—a study of carp worthy of an ichthyology textbook.

*Pu Ju (China)*—Also known as Pu Hsin-yu, Pu Ju was a master calligrapher and poet of twentieth-century China. A member of the

Ch'ing dynasty imperial family, Pu turned to painting (he was educated in science in Germany) after the overthrow of the Imperial Court
by the Chinese Republicans. He devoted himself to studying the great
calligraphy masters and created excellent copies of their styles. Pu's
dedication to calligraphy, poetry, and painting enabled him to excel
at traditional Chinese landscapes, which include thoughtful poems in
exquisite calligraphy. Many of his works are on display at the National
Palace Museum in Taipei, Taiwan.

*Kitagawa Utamaro (Japan)*—A genius of the
"ukiyo-e" (floating world) Japanese school of
woodblock printmaking, Utamaro specialized
in the prostitutes and waitresses of Yoshiwara,
the entertainment district of feudal Tokyo.
Utamaro's paintings are frozen slices of daily
life in the Japan of the late eighteenth and early
nineteenth centuries. Previous artists had
always shown entire bodies in their paintings;
Utamaro broke with tradition and painted full-face or half-body por-
traits. Because Utamoro's works were blockprints, many were pro-
duced and can be seen in a number of museums. Reproductions of his
works often decorate playing cards in Japan.

*Katsushika Hokusai* (Japan, 1760-
1849)—Famous for his "Thirty-Seven
Views of Fuji," Hokusai's elaborately
composed paintings can be found in
museums, on calendars, and on postage stamps. His painting of "The Great
Wave Off Kanagawa" has been widely
reproduced. Although Hokusai painted animals, humans, and supernatural themes, his landscapes featuring Mount Fuji established landscape as a major theme for the first time in Japanese painting. Hokusai
was a student of the great painter Shunsho, who eventually kicked
young Hokusai out of his school for exhibiting unbridled originality.

# Stupas, Pagodas, and Torii—Relief for the Stupa-fied Traveler

Three architectural forms that the observant traveler cannot miss in Asia are the stupa, pagoda, and torii—all of Indian origin. Stupas and pagodas are associated with Indian and Chinese Buddhism, respectively. Torii are the Japanese Shinto version of Buddhist gates found in India.

The Buddhist stupa is a rounded mound erected over sacred relics or sites. Buddhists adapted the form from early burial mounds and began erecting the structures over sanctuaries filled with holy relics (primarily bone fragments of the Buddha). The stupa became a symbol of the Buddha's nirvana (death).

The stupa also serves as a symbolic representation of the universe. The hemispherical dome (anda) represents the arching blue vault of the heavens. The stone umbrellas (chatravali) at the top represent the succession of heavens rising into a transcendental absolute. The mound is usually surrounded by a stone parapet (vedika) that encloses the sacred ground inside. Gates (torana) positioned at the four points of the compass allow visitors through the parapet. Between the stone fence and the stupa mound there is a processional path upon which it is customary to walk around the stupa in a clockwise direction—in the same direction as the stars move. Moving in harmony with the universe—keeping one's right shoulder turned toward the stupa—is a sign of reverence.

Probably influenced by the thirteen-storied, wooden superstructure atop a great stupa near Peshawar, India, the Chinese Buddhists began building multistoried towers at their new temples. They called them "pagodas," possibly after "dagoba," the Sinhalese (Ceylon) word for stupa. The adoption of this type of structure was easy for the Chinese who had been building pagoda-like guard towers long before Buddhism began to trickle into China in the first century A.D. Although destroyed long ago, the first pagoda on record was built near Nanjing in the third century A.D.

Like the multitiered umbrella above the Indian stupa, the different stories or levels of a pagoda represent the various levels of the Buddhist heaven. Towers can be square, round, or octagonal (the eight sides representing the Eightfold Path we will discuss under "Buddhism") in shape. Pagodas accompanied Buddhism to Korea and Japan.

Torii are seen at the entrance of every Shinto shrine in Japan. A simple gate of logs, the torii purifies the bodies of those who walk under it. The word "torii" ("bird perch") is derived from the Indian word "torana." Looking very much like a bird perch, the torii symbolically supports a cock whose crowing expels darkness from those who pass under the torii, much as the cock's crowing at dawn announces the passing of the night.

Indian torii (torana), such as those surrounding the Sanchi stupa, have three crossbars on top, while Japanese torii have only two crossbars. Although not quite as common in China, two-crossbar torii can be seen surrounding some temples in China. You will see many styles of torii in Japan—here are three of the most notable.

 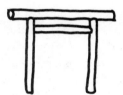 

Kuroki Torii— The original style made of round logs.

Shimmei Torii— The style used at the famous Ise Shrine.

Myojin Torii— The most common style found in Japan.

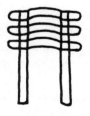

Indian Torana

# Sites—Stupas

*Sanchi, India*—The best-preserved example of the classical, large Indian stupa is found at this site in Madhya Pradesh. A brick and wood stupa was erected here during the Maurya period (400-188 B.C.) but was greatly enlarged by the subsequent Sunga and Andhra rulers. The toranas of stupa I (there are three at the site) are richly carved and show relief carvings of even earlier stupas.

*Anuradhapura, Sri Lanka*—The Jetavanarama dagoba here is the largest stupa in the world—larger than all but two of the Egyptian pyramids. It was begun in the third century A.D. Note that stupas are called "dagobas" in Sri Lanka.

*Borobudur, Indonesia*—This is the big one—2 million cubic feet of stupa. The huge, 1,100-year-old stupa of Borobudur reveals the last stage in the evolution of the stupa. By the time Buddhism reached the island of Java, the stupa had developed into a series of terraces—each terrace featuring many small stupas. The multitude of small stupas form a hemispherical mountain with a central stupa at the peak.

# Sites—Pagodas of China

*Jade Spring Temple, Hubei Province*—The Iron Pagoda on the cliff east of the temple is the best preserved iron pagoda in Asia. Thirteen stories high and made entirely of iron, the pagoda was cast in A.D. 1061 during the Northern Sung dynasty.

*Xingshengjiao Temple Pagoda, Shanghai*—Built during the Northern Sung dynasty (circa A.D. 1070), this nine-story wood and brick structure is one of the oldest buildings in this huge city. It still has more than half of its original wooden support brackets.

*Sakyamuni Pagoda of Fogong Temple, Shanxi*—This nine-story pagoda in the town of Yingxian is the tallest wooden building extant in China. The pagoda was built in A.D. 1056 during the Liao dynasty.

*Songyue Temple Pagoda, Henan*—Built in the sixth century A.D., this forty-meter-high pagoda is the oldest surviving brick pagoda in China. Its pinecone shape is very unusual.

## Sites—Pagodas of Korea and Japan

*Horyuji Pagoda, Nara, Japan*—Originally built in A.D. 607 (rebuilt in A.D. 670), the five-storied Horyuji Pagoda is part of the oldest existing temple in Japan—and is one of the oldest existing wooden structures in the world.

*Pagoda Park, Seoul, South Korea*—The ten-storied Wongaksa Pagoda in this crowded public park dates from A.D. 1466 during the Koryo dynasty.

*Pulguk-sa Temple near Kyongju, South Korea*—Sokka-t'ap and Tabo-t'ap, the two multitiered pagodas here, are the best examples of Silla kingdom pagoda architecture.

## Chinese versus Japanese Architecture

Traditional Japanese buildings are constructed of wood, because the island nation was (and is) well supplied with forests. Wooden buildings also are better than stone in being able to withstand the frequent earthquakes that rock Japan. China, with fewer earthquakes than Japan and more rock suitable for building, has a greater number of traditional stone and brick structures.

The most striking difference between the buildings of Japan and China is their color. Chinese temples and palaces almost always are painted bright vermilion and gold, while Japan relies upon the natural beauty of wood, tile, tatami (straw mats), and white rice paper. Only a few of Japan's shrines and temples (those dating from the introduction of Buddhism) are painted bright colors. The Chinese penchant for brightly painted temples may be due to the scarcity of quality wood in China—painting helped to hide the flaws and preserve the wood.

Because Buddhism and Buddhist architectural styles came through China to Japan (often by way of Korea), Chinese influences are seen in Japanese buildings—but not vice versa. I have never seen a traditional Japanese building in China. In Japan the best way to determine whether you are looking at a pure Japanese style or one influenced by the Chinese is to look for curved lines. If the roof and other structures are straight, or nearly straight, you are looking at pure Japan. If the curves are exaggerated, you are seeing the influence of China. In Japanese architecture the lack of elaborate curves and decoration, as well as the absence of bright colors, reflects the Japanese love for simplicity and refinement.

**Types of Japanese Roofs: from left to right, Hogyo, Kirizuma, Irimoya, (unique to Japan), Shichu**

---

# Sites—Japanese Architecture

*Ise-Daijingu, Ise, Japan*—Here you will find the purest example of traditional Japanese architecture, as well as the most sacred location in Japan. Although the cypress wood shrine is torn down and completely reconstructed every twenty-one years, the ancient style is faithfully maintained in minute detail. The old shrine wood is cut up and sold as charms.

# 2

# Buddhism

Thailand, Burma, Sri Lanka, and Tibet[1] are largely Buddhist states, and the religion is a strong influence in China, Japan, Korea, Cambodia, Vietnam, and Laos. Buddhism has almost disappeared from India, the land of its birth.

The Buddha (Enlightened One) was Siddhartha Gautama, who lived in the fifth century B.C., the son of royalty in a state that is now part of Nepal. Siddhartha married and had a son but was unhappy despite the many conveniences he enjoyed as a prince. At age 29, he left his privileged life behind to become a wandering ascetic in search of the Truth. He tried to find inner peace through Hindu asceticism and mind control, but failing this, he decided to find his own way to salvation.

Under a bodhi tree at Bodh Gaya, India, Siddhartha attained enlightenment (nirvana) and began to travel throughout northern India, preaching and gathering disciples. It was during this period that Siddhartha became known as the Buddha.

1. Tibet was forcibly incorporated into China in 1959.

## Four Noble Truths and an Eightfold Path

The Truth (dharma) that the Buddha discovered included four conclusions known as the Four Noble Truths, which are listed below.

1. Humans suffer and are dissatisfied.

2. Unfulfilled desire causes suffering. We are unfulfilled because we always desire more of everything. We want more money, more love, more power, etc. Ego is at the root of desire.

3. The fulfillment that humans want cannot be satisfied by outside factors such as money and power. Satisfaction comes only from within—and from a source that is not transitory.

4. The key to this source is self-knowledge, and self-knowledge is attained by following the Eightfold Path:

Right belief

Right feelings (wisdom)

Right speech

Right actions (morality)

Right livelihood

Right endeavor

Right memory (mental discipline)

Right meditation

By following the Eightfold Path, one can attain a state of nirvana (literally, "blowing out"), the extinguishing of the flame of desire. Nirvana is not death. It is, rather, a state of supreme bliss. The Buddha taught that each individual must discover his own way to nirvana.

## The Great Schism

The Buddha never wrote down his teachings, and after his death (about 480 B.C.), doctrinal disputes erupted and corrupted some of his teachings. Contrary to the Buddha's instructions, some of his followers began to deify him. His teachings became an established religion, complete with ornate rituals that sometimes took precedence over the Buddha's original moral teachings.

The disputes eventually led to a great schism among Buddhists in the first century A.D. Reformers established a new school of Buddhism, which sought to popularize the faith by establishing the Buddha as a savior to be worshiped by allowing his representation in human form (he had previously been represented only by symbols), and by teaching that nirvana was attainable by everyone—not just reclusive monks. The reformers called their school of Buddhism the Mahayana or "Great Vehicle." Because the Mahayana gained acceptance in Nepal, Tibet, China, Korea, and Japan, it is also known as the "northern church."

The orthodox school survived and continues to thrive in Sri Lanka, Thailand, Burma, and Singapore. Generally known by the name of the largest of its eighteen sects, the Theravada school (Mahayana Budd-

hists prefer to call it the Hinayana, or "Lesser Vehicle"), its faithful see
the Buddha as a mortal who showed the way by discovering the Four
Noble Truths and the Eightfold Path. No deity is worshiped in Theravada Buddhism, and salvation must be worked out by each
individual.

In contrast to Theravada doctrine, the northern school believes that
its adherents may ask the Buddha to intervene in their lives. The
Mahayana also adopted a pantheon of celestial beings, including bodhisattvas, beings who could attain nirvana but who decide to remain
in the world to help humans find the way. The bodhisattvas are
accompanied by specialized Buddhas who control various regions of
the universe.

The contrast between Theravada and Mahayana is most evident in
the arts. There is a strong streak of puritanism in Theravada art. Any
hint of sensuality or artistic expressionism is frowned upon by the
orthodox Theravadan. Some extravagance of color is tolerated if by
such compromise the simpleminded can be led to the truth symbolized
in the art. In contrast, Mahayana temples are resplendent with ornate
statues and reliefs of the numerous, and often terrifying, Buddhas and
bodhisattvas.

In India, the land of its origin, Buddhism gradually became
absorbed into Hinduism. Hindus even made the Buddha the ninth
incarnation of the Hindu god Vishnu. The final blow came with the
Islamic invasion of India in the twelfth century. The new Muslim
rulers of northern India destroyed the centers of Buddhist teaching and
razed most of the great monuments of Buddhism. Today, fewer than
1 percent of Indians are Buddhist.

The success of Buddhism outside of India, however, helped to carry
Indic civilization to many foreign lands. Many Chinese words in use
today are corruptions of transliterated Sanskrit words of Buddhist origin. Although most Chinese who use these words do not realize it, they
are helping to keep alive a little bit of ancient India.

## The Samurai Connection

In sixth-century China, a new branch of Buddhism took root, stressing
that the release from desire and suffering came through introspection

and a phased program of discipline and meditation. Chan ("Zen" in Japanese) Buddhism gained popularity among the elite of T'ang China and was introduced to Japan during that country's rage for things Chinese. Zen Buddhism found favor with the discipline-loving military orders of Japan—the samurai. Few modern Japanese practice Zen, or any other form of Buddhism. Although traces of Buddhist culture run throughout contemporary Japanese society (most Japanese are buried with a Buddhist ceremony), Japan has become increasingly secularized during the last three centuries.

## Buddhist Art

Virtually all images of the Buddha are copies of previous Buddha images. The positions, gestures, and features remain virtually unchanged, because to alter these traditions could diminish the special power of the symbolism. The closer an image resembles the original model, the more the original's power is preserved. Artists who expressed their own personal view of the Buddha would not have found any patrons. When looking at various representations of the Buddha, remember that their purpose is not to present a portrait but to make spiritual qualities visible. The artistic beauty of the Buddhas is entirely incidental to their function as devotional images.

In accordance with Buddhist iconography of second-century India, the Buddha's physical appearance is usually distinguished by six traditional features:

1. His body proportions must be harmonious (broad shoulders, narrow hips).
2. His arms must be smooth and round.
3. His fingertips should be bent back.
4. His hair must fall in short locks curled to the right.
5. His earlobes must be long.
6. His face must be oval-shaped.

### Understanding Buddhist Iconography

When you understand why the Buddha has a bump on his head, you will have attained enlightenment (at least in regard to Buddhist iconography). The bump, the hand gestures, and other recurring characteristics of traditional Buddhist symbols are full of meaning.

By the time Indian and central Asian Buddhist missionaries brought Buddhism to China in the second century A.D., their religious art had acquired fairly standardized symbols (iconography). The characteristics to look for can be placed into three categories: hand gestures; leg positions; and everything else.

*Hand Gestures (mudra)*[2]

Keep your eyes on the Buddha's hands—there is some serious body language going on there, and they will tell you exactly what he is saying. Each hand position (mudra) has its own terminology. For example, the following positions are likely to be seen:

The *bhumisparsamudra* or earth-touching gesture is the most popular way of portraying the Buddha. The Buddha is shown sitting cross-legged with his left palm upward in his lap and his right hand over his right knee with the fingertips touching the ground. The fingers touching the ground symbolizes the Buddha calling on the earth to bear witness to his enlightenment and right to the throne of knowledge.

In the *dhyanamudra* gesture, the Buddha has his opened hands in his lap, one above the other, signifying that he is in meditation.

2. The original Indian Sanskrit terms for the positions are still used.

For the *varamudra* hand position, the Buddha's left hand is turned downward with the palm exposed. This gesture symbolizes charity or giving.

The Buddha reassures the world with the gesture of *abhayamudra*, His right hand is raised with the palm outwards in this gesture of granting protection or absence of fear. If the Buddha is standing, his left hand will usually point down with the palm outward to symbolize the giving of blessings.

Here are some other popular hand gestures and their meanings:

If the Buddha's hands are raised to his chest, the Buddha is being depicted at his first sermon, telling the world of his discovery of enlightenment.

If his hand is turned downward with the palm towards his body, this symbolizes favor-granting by the Buddha.

*Leg Positions*

The positioning of the Buddha's legs also packs meaning. Watch for
the following common positions:

   In the position known as *lalitasana*, one leg is shown pulled up next
to the body while the other hangs down to the ground; this indicates
relaxation.

   *Dhyanasana*, shows the legs pulled up next to the body, feet atop
each other in the lap; this is the classic pose of meditation.

   In *maharajalilasana*, the Buddha holds one leg vertically against the
body, and the other lies horizontally on the ground. This is known as
the posture of royal ease.

## Head Bumps and Lotus-Flowers

The round bump often topped with a flame or lotus-bud on the crown of the Buddha's head is called the *usnisa* and symbolizes enlightenment. The additional cranial room provided by the *usnisa* was needed to contain the knowledge the Buddha attained at enlightenment. That hole or bump in the middle of the Buddha's forehead, from which an illuminating ray of light is emitted, is called the *urna*. With this symbolic beam of light, the Buddha forces darkness from the world.

At the base of Buddha statues one usually finds a stylized lotus-flower; this symbolizes man's "Buddha-nature," which remains untouched by the filth of earthly existence. The lotus also symbolizes spontaneous generation and therefore the Buddha's divine birth.

## Body Language

The Buddha can be represented in four positions (standing, sitting, walking, or reclining). As with other dignified religious figures, the Buddha is never shown running, skipping, or moon-walking. The Buddha is usually seated with his legs horizontal, one leg atop the other. If the Buddha is presented as lying on his right side with his head resting on his right hand, this symbolizes his death and passage into nirvana.

The Buddha is usually shown with relaxed muscles and peaceful features to indicate his calm state of enlightenment.

As we have discussed, the Mahayana school of Buddhism developed a doctrine that called for more than one Buddha and introduced a host of bodhisattvas—beings who have attained enlightment but put off entrance to nirvana in order to help mankind.

Distinguishing the many Buddhas and bodhisattvas from one another is not easy, but hand gestures often give a clue. The historical Buddha (Siddhartha) usually displays the *abhayamudra* gesture of reassurance described above—hand raised with palm outward. Bhaisajyaguru, the Buddha able to cure sickness, is almost always portrayed holding a medicine pot in his left hand.

Bodhisattvas are often portrayed as attendants to a Buddha. It is very common to see a Buddha flanked on either side by bodhisattvas. An ornate crown, perhaps similar to the one worn by Siddhartha when he was still a member of the Indian nobility, is usually a giveaway of bodhisattvahood. Also look for lots of jewelry and flowing silk garments on bodhisattvas.

The most popular bodhisattva underwent a sex change toward the end of the first millennium A.D. Kuanyin, the Goddess of Mercy in China (called Kwannon in Japan), was at first represented as a man but he gradually assumed female characteristics. The Chinese apparently preferred their god of mercy to be a goddess—mercy being a quality more closely associated with females. Kuanyin usually holds a bottle containing the nectar of immortality; on other occasions she holds a lotus flower. In Japan she has developed extra arms and heads as well. In Taiwan her birthday is celebrated as a holiday on the nineteenth day of the second lunar month. Kuanyin should not take her popularity for granted, however—the faithful have been known to change allegiance quite suddenly. Consider Maitreya, the Buddha of the Future. He was the most popular Buddha in early Buddhist China, but was soon displaced by Amituo, the compassionate Buddha in charge of the Western Paradise.

The fierce-looking beings often prominent around Buddhist temples in Japan and Korea are guardians of the Buddhist realm. They are not Buddhas or bodhisattvas but are nevertheless indispensable in the fight against evil, and they carry swords, ropes, and assorted weapons to help in that struggle. These fierce fellows usually come in fours (to protect the four quarters of the universe) and fives (the fifth to protect the center).

## Temple Strategy

A few years ago, I watched a group of camera-wielding Westerners get off a tour bus at my hotel in Kyoto. They looked numb, their eyes focused on the carpet. There was very little of the usual chatter as they shuffled off to their rooms, but one elderly lady in a happi coat caught my eye, and with a look of grim desperation, as if she wanted to make her last breath count, she gasped, "If I see one more cotton-pickin' temple I'm going to go berserk!"

Research has shown that the average tourist's brain locks up when subjected to more than three temples per day. Pace yourself when you

**Kuanyin, or Kwannon, Goddess of Mercy**

go temple-hopping. Know when to say when. If you expend your curiosity and energy in the beginning on unremarkable temples and shrines, you may never make it to to the real masterpieces. In Japan the temple-laden cities of Kyoto and Nara are especially hazardous to the nonselective traveler. Here are some remarkable, easy-to-get-to Buddhist temples.

**Peking (Beijing)**

Lama Temple
Temple of the White Dagoba
Temple of Heaven

**Taipei**

Lungshan Temple

BUDDHIST TEMPLE OF IKEGAMI

**Bangkok**

Wat Phra Keo
Wat Pho
Wat Traimit
Phra Pathom Chedi

**Tokyo**

Gotokuji Temple
Asakusa Sensoji Temple

# Sites—Buddhism

*Anuradhapura, Sri Lanka*—This was the capital of Sri Lanka when Buddhism was brought to the island by Indians. One of Buddhism's most sacred spots is found here in the ruins of King Devanampiyatissa's garden. The son of an Indian ruler planted here a cutting of the bodhi tree under which the Buddha achieved enlightenment. The original bodhi tree in India no longer exists, but the transplant in Sri Lanka continues to thrive. You will also find here a number of stupas—the mounds that serve as Buddhist shrines. Some of them rival in height the dome of St. Peter's at the Vatican.

*Temple of the Tooth, Kandy, Sri Lanka*—The Buddha's revered left eyetooth is enshrined here. The holy relic already was more than 800 years old when brought to Sri Lanka in the fourth century A.D. The tooth is encased within several gold caskets, so all you can say is that you were close to it.

After you have seen the best, then by all means see the rest.

# 3

# Hinduism

There are more than 600 million Hindus in the world, and most of them live in India, the land of the religion's origin. Hinduism has had an impact far beyond India, however, especially in Southeast Asia. The traveler can find the Hindu culture alive and kicking as far away as Bali in Indonesia. Hinduism differs from Buddhism (and most other religions) in that it did not have a founder figure—there is no historical equivalent to the Buddha (Siddhartha Gautama) in Hinduism. Nor is there a church or governing body. Hinduism is as much a way of life as it is a religion.

The origin of Hinduism is a good deal murkier than the other major religions. The genesis seems to lie in the clashing and subsequent synthesis between the ancient Indus Valley culture and Aryan invaders. The Aryans entered the Indus Valley region (present-day Pakistan) in the second millennium B.C., and within centuries, a distinct culture evolved that integrated characteristics of both the Indus Valley "mother goddess" fertility cult and the Aryan ideology.

By 500 B.C. the tenets and mythology of this distinct culture is recognizable as what we call Hinduism. It was still pretty elastic theologically, but there were some basic beliefs that served as a starting point.

A class or caste system had been adopted by the Brahmans, the priests who guided the faithful. Not surprisingly, the Brahmans had established themselves at the top of the hierarchy—followed by warriors and nobility, artisans and traders, and at the bottom, the serfs. The most unfortunate class became a "nonclass"—the untouchables.

There is no single sacred text in Hinduism which could be equated with the Christian Bible or the Muslim Koran. There are a number of epics and tracts that are used as the basis for Hindu teachings, however. Texts such as the *Upanishads* (ca. 500 B.C.) and the *Mahabharata* were created by learned poets and practitioners of the faith. The themes expressed in these texts convey the substance of Hinduism and set forth the moral duties (dharma) to be observed.

The Hindu believes that all living things have souls, and that all of these souls have equal merit. Some of these souls would seem to be more equal than others—based upon a balance sheet of the soul's good vs. bad deeds. The accounting system is based upon "karma," the code of consequences. If a soul has accumulated sufficient merit by observance of dharma, it is able to progress toward "moksha," or release from its earthbound restrictions, into the true peace of the world-soul (Brahmam).

Until the soul achieves moksha, it is bound up in a cycle of birth and rebirth—going from one life-form to another. Whether one is reborn as a noble or a parasite (or both) depends upon the status of one's karma at the time of the body's death. This doctrine of birth and rebirth (samsara) has a major effect upon the lives of most Hindus. If one is mired in poverty and low caste, there is always hope, at least in the next life.

The system of castes is still widely observed despite the legal prohibition against discrimination. Certain subcastes (there are hundreds if not thousands of subcastes) are taking on the appearance of occupational associations rather than religiously ordained social classes. Most Hindus continue to accept the consequences of birth into a caste, although there are occasional instances of someone switching castes or becoming disassociated with caste restrictions. Still, members of different castes will seldom dine together or intermarry.

Hinduism was spread to Southeast Asia by traders and priests rather than by soldiers. It caught on and reached its height in the Khmer kingdoms of Angkor. Hindu spirituality permeated every aspect of Angkor—from the political and social systems to the shape of the great temples. Hindu symbolism is everywhere to be seen at Angkor Wat in Cambodia.

## Hindu Cosmology and the Temple

There are two major Hindu theories about the universe. According to one theory, the universe is a "cosmic egg" divided into several zones, one of which humans occupy. The most popular theory, however, is that the universe is flat and circular. In the center of this flat universe rises Mount Meru, home of the gods. Several continents and oceans encircle the mountain. Humans are said to live on the "rose-apple continent" after the primary flora of the land.

Throughout the realm of Hindu influence, particularly in Southeast Asia, monuments are built that reflect this cosmological scheme. Since the function of the Hindu temple is to bring the gods and man together, the temple is designed as a facsimile of the dwelling place of the gods (Mount Meru) and the surrounding universe. The tiered tower rising above each temple is specifically identified with Mout Meru and is literally called the "mountaintop" (shikhara).

Nothing in the layout of a Hindu temple is unplanned. All dimensions and proportions are determined by an exacting system that utilizes mathematics to create an expression of the universe. The placement of every niche and every door is an integral part of a sacred geometry about which whole textbooks are devoted. The images and symbols within a temple both represent certain gods and are designed to function as a receptacle for the god to take up residence in. Traditionally, if the images and symbols within the temple are not created in exacting, prescribed proportions, worshiping them is a waste of time—a diety will not reside in an imperfect image.

The center of the temple corresponds with the center of the universe. The image or symbol of the major diety is placed at this most sacred point in the temple. The rest of the temple is planned according to a square that is drawn around the center. The square is then subdivided into a number of smaller squares that represent different areas of the universe. Because each part of the universe has its own presiding deities, their images are placed within their respective portions of the universe as it is recreated in the form of the temple.

The Hindu has always placed a high priority on the propagation of life and the survival of the family. Fertility is therefore a topic of interest and is often the subject of Hindu artisans. The English colonizers were scandalized by what they found upon Hindu temple walls—and to-day's Western visitor is often surprised. The sight of erotic female images posturing over doorways, the imaginative depictions of sexual intercourse—and even acts of sexual deviation—often leave unprepared tourists tittering and red-faced. To the Hindu, however, eroticism has always been auspicious and symbolic of the continuance of the community—and thus connected with the protection of the temple. Erotic motifs are frequently found near the temple doorways, where the temple is most vulnerable to the invasion of evil forces.

Temple styles reflect the cultural differences between northern and southern India. Southern temples typically have a moulded plinth and overhanging eaves. The seventh-century Meguti Temple at Aihole and the ninth-century Brihadeshvara Temple at Tanjore are good examples of southern-style temples. Great, walled temple complexes became popular in south India. Many could be mistaken for walled fortresses.

---

# Sites—Hindu Temples

*Khajuraho, India*—The twenty-two Temples in this town (the religious capital of a tenth- to twelfth-century kingdom) display what must be the world's largest collection of erotic art. Many theories exist to explain the builders' interest in eroticism, but the most popular is simply that sexuality was deemed auspicious because it is bound up with procreation and the survival of the community. Today's Indian authorities are not as broad-minded as their ancestors—close-up photography of the carved "alasa kanyas" (languid maidens) is prohibited in some temples. The Lakshmana Temple here is the best preserved temple, and the sculptures exhibit an extraordinary tactile quality.

# Hinduism's Classics

The *Ramayana* and *Mahabharata* are the two great national epics of Hindu India. The traveler should be familiar with these works if he or she is to understand much of the art seen in India and Southeast Asia. The numerous subplots of the epics have become a part of the life of the people and are played out on reliefs and in dance performances from India to Indonesia.

The *Ramayana* tells of events around 1000 B.C., but the early versions of these works have been lost. Fifth-century B.C. Gupta writers wrote the versions that survive today. Becoming familiar with the *Mahabharata* is about all most of us can hope for, since it is more than 220,000 lines in length—more than seven times as long as the *Iliad* and the *Odyssey* combined!

## The Ramayana

The 48,000-line *Ramayana* is the more commonly encountered of the two epics. The story may be given different names (the Thais call it "Ramakien") and the details changed to reflect local folk culture, but the moral of the story remains the same: good wins out over evil—but only after a struggle.

To understand the *Ramayana*, it is necessary to understand the Hindu god Vishnu. Vishnu has several incarnations, three of which are Desartharama (Rama), Krishna, and the Buddha. Many of you may have heard the Hare Krishnas chanting "Rama Rama, Krishna, Krishna." Rama's popularity took off when the Indian poet Valmiki penned the *Ramayana* and made him the superhero of the fifth century B.C. tale of adventure.

The *Ramayana*'s cast includes:

Rama—eldest son of King Dasharatha and incarnation of Vishnu
Ayodhya—The land that King Dasharatha ruled
Sita—Rama's wife
Lakshmana—Rama's younger brother
Ravana—The ten-headed demon king of Lanka (Ceylon)
Hanumana—The leader of an army of pro-Rama monkeys.

In a nutshell, the story is as follows. The blue-faced (symbolizing bravery) Rama wins his wife Sita by winning a bow-stringing contest.

They are a happy couple at the Ayodhya palace for twelve years, until Rama's jealous stepmother gets them exiled to the forest. In the forest, Rama rejects the amorous advances of Ravana's (the demon king of Lanka) ugly sister by lopping off her nose and breasts. Upset, Ravana has Sita carried off to Lanka by his army of fiends and demons. Rama and his monkey allies rescue her by building a bridge between India and Lanka with chunks of the Himalaya Mountains. The reunited Rama and Sita return to their Solar dynasty of Oudh for a long and success-ful reign.

## Sites—Ramayana

*Ayodhya, Uttar Pradesh, India*—The day after the Indian festival of Holi (day after the March full moon), Rama's birthday is celebrated by thousands of pil-grims, who converge on the temples in the city thought to be Rama's birthplace. Images of the *Ramayana* characters are carried about in processions.

### The Mahabharata

The *Mahabharata* epic revolves around a family feud between the Pan-dava brothers and their Kaurava cousins. Irritated by the Kauravas' usurpation of their throne, the formerly royal Pandavas enlist the aid of Krishna, an earthly incarnation of Vishnu, to regain their kingdom. Plans are made for the counterattack, but Arjuna, the commander of the Pandava forces, balks at attacking members of his family. At this crucial point, Krishna jumps in to persuade Arjuna to do his duty. Arjuna's questioning of Krishna about right and wrong and Krishna's battlefield discourse on "dharma" (duty or code) form the fragment of the *Mahabharata* known as the *Bhagavad-Gita* (Lord's Song).

Krishna reveals the four ways to achieve enlightenment: the paths of "karma" (work), "bhakti" (devotion), "jnana" (knowledge), and "yoga" (meditation). Krishna goes on to cover the do's and don'ts of almost every conceivable situation in life.

# 4

# Islam

Pakistan, Afghanistan, Brunei, Malaysia, and Indonesia are Islamic nations. Although Islam originated on the Arabian Peninsula, the faith quickly spread and has had tremendous impact in Asia. Indonesia alone is home to more Muslims than any Arab nation. These Islamic nations of Asia cannot be understood without understanding Islam.

The religion of Islam (literally, "submission") was founded in A.D. 610 by Muhammad, in what is now known as Saudi Arabia. At age forty, he began having visions in which an angel commanded him to begin proselytizing the new religion. The residents of Mecca, Muhammad's hometown, were not impressed—they ran him out of town as a quack. Muhammad proved to be persuasive, however, and eight years later he led an army of followers back to Mecca and took the city by force. Ever since then, Mecca has been the center of Islam and the focus of prayer for the Muslim world.

Although Muslims ("Mohammedans" is considered insulting) accept the revelations of Christian prophets such as Abraham and Jesus, Muhammad is believed to be "the Prophet," the one to whom God delivered complete and perfect revelations. These revelations are set forth in the Koran (Qur'an), the principal scripture of Islam.

## The Five Pillars of Faith

Islam is strictly a monotheistic faith. There is only one God (Allah). At the core of Islam stand the Five Pillars:

1. The Attestation of Faith: "There is no god but God, and Muhammad is His messenger."
2. Prayer five times a day, at sunrise, noon, mid-afternoon, sunset, and nightfall.
3. Fasting and abstinence from smoking and sex, from sunrise to sunset during the Muslim month of Ramadan.
4. Giving of alms to the poor.
5. Pilgrimage (hajj) to Mecca at least once a lifetime for any Muslim who can afford it.

Within a century after Muhammad's death, much of the territory from Spain to the border of China was conquered by Islamic armies. Islam reached India in the eighth century but did not take hold until the twelfth century, when it was forced on the subcontinent by Muslim rulers. Today there are more than 400 million Muslims worldwide.

## Mecca—Center of Islam

The focus of the Muslim's prayers and the destination of his pilgrimage is a hollow, fifty-foot-high, stone-and-mortar cube in Mecca called the Kaaba ("cube" in Arabic). A sacred place to the Arabs long before Muhammad's time, the Kaaba is believed to be directly under Allah's throne and to be the center of creation. When the millions of Muslims throughout the world turn toward Mecca five times a day for prayer, they are symbolically uniting at the Kaaba.

Within each mosque, there is an arched niche (*mihrab*) in one wall that indicates the direction of Mecca. During prayer, Muslims can use the *mihrab* to align themselves with the Kaaba in Mecca. The arched niche of the *mihrab* is a motif frequently seen in Islamic art and on the prayer rugs carried by many Muslims as portable oratories.

The imaginary line stretching between the worshiper and the Kaaba (through the *mihrab*) is called the "kibla" and is seen as a kind of umbilical cord linking the worshiper with the source of creation (the Kaaba) and, by extension, with Allah above. The Kaaba, *kibla*, and worshiper form a spoked wheel with the hub in Mecca.

Muslims from throughout the world travel each year to Mecca (non-Muslims are not permitted in the city) to pay homage to Allah. They do this by circling the Kaaba seven times in a counterclockwise direction.

## Manifestations of the Faith

Islam is a very conservative religion. The sexes are separated for most religious activities, and women are generally restricted to the home. Eating pork is taboo. All males undergo compulsory circumcision at puberty.

In contrast to Buddhism and Hinduism, Islam has been generally intolerant of other faiths within their midst. Proselytizing to Muslims by other religions is forbidden in most Islamic states, including those in Asia. In India, thousands of Hindu and Buddhist sacred sites and temples were torn down by Muslim rulers of that country. Some of the greatest mosques in northern India were constructed of material torn from Hindu temples.

Islam, like Buddhism, suffered a great schism after its founder's death. The Sunni branch favored election of the head of the faith, while the Shi'ites wanted the leader to be appointed. The division was never resolved, and the two main sects divide the faith today.

Muslims observe a twelve-month lunar calendar, which is ten days shorter than the Western Gregorian calendar. The months begin and end with the new moon and are twenty-nine or thirty days long.

## Islamic Art

Even the casual viewer of Islamic decorative art will notice the Muslim love for repeating geometrically complex patterns. The Arabs excelled at astronomy and mathematics (we use their Arabic numerals today) and applied their fondness for geometry to their art.

The mosques and mausoleums of Islam do not contain human

images—Muslims believe that to mimic the creations of Allah would be blasphemous. Nor will you find in mosques any representation of Allah either, symbolic or realistic. Only outside the religious realm does Islam allow the representation of people and animals.

Visitors to mosques will note the extreme simplicity of the architecture. The mosque is intended to separate worshipers from the spiritual pollution of the external world and allow them to concentrate on prayer; the result is an absence of decorative distraction.

## Sites—Islam

*Kutb Mosque, Delhi, India*—Built in A.D. 1193, this mosque is the earliest surviving example of Islamic architecture in India. Kutb Mosque is dominated by a 240-foot high, ribbed minaret (the Kutb Manar), set in front of a large *mihrab* in a crumbling wall. Both the walls and the minaret are covered with finely carved reliefs. The mosque was constructed from the remains of a destroyed Jain temple.

*Masjid Negara, Kuala Lumpur, Malaysia*—This modern national mosque of Malaysia is beautiful in its simplicity. Gleaming white domes and minaret lend an atmosphere of purity to this airy mosque, which can accommodate thousands of worshipers. A serene pool surrounds the minaret. Non-Muslims are allowed to enter the mosque before 2 p.m., except Fridays.

# II.

# History and Culture

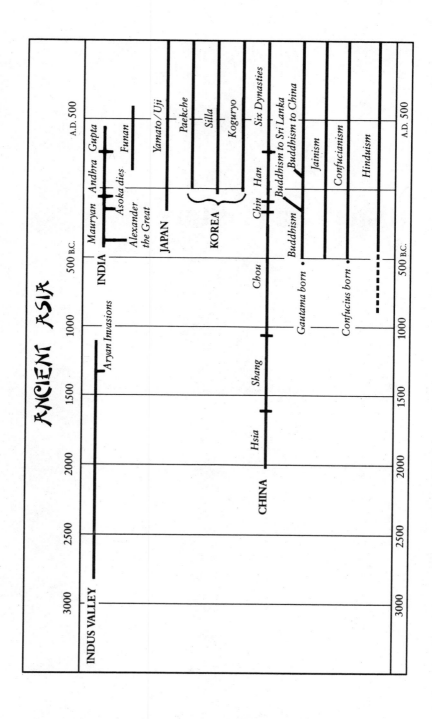

# ANCIENT ASIA

| | 3000 | 2500 | 2000 | 1500 | 1000 | 500 B.C. | A.D. 500 |
|---|---|---|---|---|---|---|---|

**INDUS VALLEY**

**INDIA**

Aryan Invasions

Mauryan · Andhra · Gupta
Asoka dies
Alexander the Great
Funan

**JAPAN**

Yamato / Uji

**KOREA**

Paekche
Silla
Koguryo

**CHINA**

Hsia
Shang
Chou
Chin · Han · Six Dynasties

Gautama born ·
Buddhism
Buddhism to Sri Lanka
Buddhism to China

Confucius born ·
Jainism
Confucianism

Hinduism

# 5

# Ancient Asia
# (3000 B.C.—A.D. 500)

## Start at the Mound of the Dead

The place to begin your search for the roots of Asian civilization is a fascinating town 400 miles north of Karachi, Pakistan. Moenjodaro (Mound of the Dead) is better planned than most urban centers in the region, boasting pleasantly broad, straight, perpendicular streets, an efficient sanitation system, and enormous public baths. But do not plan on staying overnight—the last four-star hostelry in Moenjodaro closed 3,500 years ago when the residents abandoned their city.[1]

Riding a bullock cart into nearby Dokri village, you can easily imagine what life must have been like for the citizens of Moenjodaro at the height of the Indus Valley civilization, circa 2000 B.C. During that period, the mostly dark-skinned inhabitants of the Indus Valley were busy molding the face of Indic (Indian) civilization. They left behind thousands of small soapstone seals that modern archaeologists have found. The seals exhibit a variety of carved animals of impressive

---

1. Air-conditioned inns can be found in nearby Larkana.

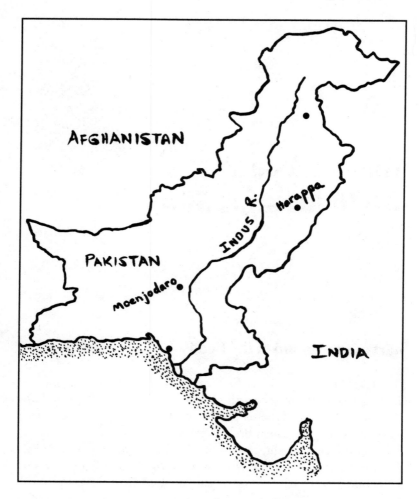

beauty and realism; many of the images (bulls, elephants, oxen, etc.)
later became powerful symbols and common motifs in Hindu art.

The Indus Valley people probably came from the hills of Baluchistan
in northwest Pakistan during the third millennium B.C. Although most
were farmers, they were familiar with the cities of Sumer in Mesopotamia. They became great traders—their products have been found in
Bahrain in the Persian Gulf and in the Mesopotamian ruins of southwest Asia.

Indus Valley culture centered around the two great cities of Moen-jodaro and Harappa (the latter situated 350 miles northeast of Moen-jodaro). Unlike the cities of other great civilizations of the time, Har-appan[2] communities were well-planned and laid out on a grid pattern. The periodically flooded and ruined cities were rebuilt as perfect copies atop these old grids. The Harappans loved bricks and used them to build streets, sewage drains, multistory houses, even garbage chutes in buildings that conveyed waste to the street for easy pickup by the sanitation department. They even made brick pipes which drained into the city's well-designed sewage system. Order pervaded the civilization. The Harappan love for orderliness is evident even in their bricks, which were made in only two sizes (9.2"x 4.5"x 2.2" and 11"x 5.5"x 2.5").

Tons of these ancient bricks were picked up and used centuries later to build the Lahore-Multan railway. And a close look at area homes would reveal that the Harappans' hard work is still paying dividends. The Harappans left abundant evidence of their written language in the form of symbols carved into clay seals, but today's archaeologists, working with computer-aided cryptographers, have been unable to decipher the mysterious Harappan text. Bulls, snakes, and swastikas (symbolizing well-being) were frequently used symbols on the seals. The Indus Valley civilization's religion seems to have been a fertility cult based on worship of the Great Mother.

## Sites—Harappan Civilization

*Moenjodaro*—The most impressive structure left of this ancient city is the Great Bath, a large, brick-lined bathing pool surrounded by galleries and verandas. An ingenious drainage system is built into this water-tight marvel. Other ruins worth seeing are the granary where the harvests were kept, the palace, and the priests' assembly center. Only brick foundations are left of these structures, but the fine workmanship and large dimensions of the ruins are enough to conjure up images of a grand city.

2. The people of the ancient Indus Valley civilization are often called Harappans, after the excavated city of Harappa, which was given the name of a modern village near the site. "Harappans" is also easier to say than "Moenjodaroians."

*Harappa*—The namesake of the Harappan civilization, this is the twin city of Moenjodaro. The museum here displays the mysterious seals and small sculptures unearthed at the site.

Note that many of the small sculptures and seals found at Moenjodaro and Harappa are on display at the National Museum of Pakistan in Karachi and at the National Museum of India in New Delhi.

---

The Indus Valley was one of five great centers of early civilization—along with the Nile Valley of Egypt, the Tigris-Euphrates river valleys of Mesopotamia, the Yellow River basin of China, and the Minoan civilization of the island of Crete. The Indus Valley civilization seems to have developed about a thousand years after the earliest known civilization—the Sumerians of Mesopotamia. During the second millennium B.C., nomadic invasions dramatically changed each of these civilizations, except that of Egypt.

## The Aryans

Between 2000 and 1500 B.C., tribes of blue-eyed, fair-skinned Indo-Europeans moved away from their homeland near the Caspian Sea. Some moved west into pre-Greek Greece and absorbed the Minoan culture of Crete. These Indo-European invaders became the seafaring Mycenaeans. The cattle herders who headed east called themselves "Aryans" or "nobles." Like all pastoral peoples, they were constantly on the lookout for better real estate for their herds. The Aryans lingered in Iran, and then small groups began creeping into the fertile Indus Valley of present-day Pakistan—where they found the Harappan cities.

Unlike the Harappans whom they eventually overwhelmed, the Aryans left behind little of permanence—with one great exception. The Aryans brought with them a sophisticated religion called Brahmanism, which when mixed with the Great Mother fertility cult of the Harappans, begat Hinduism. More than 3,000 years later, 85 percent of India's inhabitants adhere to a way of life (Hinduism) that had its origins in the Aryan religion.

The principal scriptures of the Aryan religion were the *Vedas*, collections of sacred hymns passed orally between generations. For 3,000 years, thousands of hymns were transmitted through the culture in this way. To have written down the sacred hymns would have destroyed their mysterious power. The earliest evidence of a written Vedic text is from the fifteenth century A.D.

The only picture we have of the Aryan way of life is that which they painted of themselves in the *Vedas*: they were beef-eaters, rode chariots, used an intoxicant called "soma" (it may have been hashish), and despised the Harappans, whose phallic rituals they found particularly offensive. Perhaps the most important revelation of these books is that Aryan religious rituals and symbols were very similar to those of their Indo-European cousins in ancient Iran and Greece.

Ideas about the caste system, transmigration of the soul, supremacy of the priests, and cow veneration were added by Hindus later—these doctrines were not part of early Aryan society.

## The Synthesis

The Aryans may have overwhelmed the Harappans, or Dasas (slaves), as the Aryans called them, but as it has so often happened, the victors absorbed the vanquished culture and a new, hybrid civilization arose. The Aryans and Harappans eventually began to intermarry, and Aryan adventurism, literary tradition, and language were fused with Harappan culture.

The stifling hereditary caste system still operational in much of the subcontinent was a bad fruit of this Aryan and Harappan union. The Aryans had originally divided themselves into the three classes: noble, priest, and commoner. People were not prohibited from changing classes or marrying across class lines. When the light-skinned Aryans began living near the dark-skinned Harappans, however, the Aryans acquired an acute consciousness of racial superiority and developed a system of four hereditary castes, based upon color, to prevent mixing of the races. Aryan priests (Brahmans), warrior nobles (Kshatriyas), and farmers (Vaishyas) were the three higher castes. The despised Dasas

(Harappans) were lumped together into the fourth and lowest caste. With time and intermarriage, skin color lost most of its importance as a criterion for caste membership, but the occupation of one's ancestors continued to determine the newborn's caste membership. Although discrimination has been made illegal in today's India, the caste system still functions in many areas.

## The Dravidians

Many believe that those Harappans who were not a part of the Aryan-Harappan fusion in the Indus Valley were pushed south by the invaders and made their home in south India (where their descendants are called Dravidians), in Sri Lanka (the Veddas), and possibly in Australia (the aborigines). As you travel south down the Indian peninsula past Madras, you will find their descendants. You will discover that the people of south India are generally darker and shorter than in the north. Their languages are fundamentally different from the Indo-European languages of the north. Many of these Tamil speakers (the major Dravidian language) reject the Indian government's attempts to make Hindi (the major language of the north) the official language of India. So your Hindi phrasebook can remain packed away while you are in the south.

## The Reformers—Buddhism and Jainism

By about 500 B.C. some people were feeling put out about the caste system and the privileges the priestly Brahman class had given itself. Buddhism and Jainism were founded by two sons of the noble warrior caste, who found that riches and position did not equal happiness or inner peace. Although Buddhism later became virtually extinct in India, it had a profound impact in East and Southeast Asia and Sri Lanka.

Only two of the reformed religions survived to become major religions of today. Jainism still thrives in India, but Buddhism has all but disappeared in its native land. Indian Buddhism was transferred to Tibet, China, and East Asia in time to survive. By the gift of Buddhism,

India profoundly influenced the history and society of China. China never had a similar influence upon India.

Jainism must be the world's most ascetic religion. Its adherents believe violence toward any living creature is the most heinous sin, so they go to great lengths to avoid killing anything—including insects. Their monks can be seen wearing cotton masks to avoid inhaling a hapless bug and sweeping their path with a whisk broom least they step on the crawling variety. The Jain (rhymes with "mine") believe that the soul is immortal and transmigrates from living creature to living creature.

The founder of Jainism, Mahavira, was a contemporary of the Buddha in sixth-century India. Like Buddha, Mahavira was a member of a noble family who quit the good life to become an ascetic and find enlightenment. He, too, rebelled against the caste system and the privileges of the Brahman priests. The Jains believe that Mahavira was the twenty-fourth and most recent of a line of great teachers (the "tirthankaras") that stretches back into antiquity.

Like the Buddhists, the Jains do not believe in a god or a creator of the universe. The concept of nirvana—the self-attainment of enlightenment—is also common to both religions. Where the Jains differ from the Buddhists is in their belief that only the ascetic monk can attain enlightment, while Buddhists believe nirvana is open to any who seek it.

There are two sects of Jainism: the "sky-clad," who go about naked to show their detachment from worldly life; and the less ascetic "white-clads," who wear loose-fitting white cotton clothes. Although the sky-clads are still seen in India, their numbers dwindled after the eleventh-century Muslim rulers made them wear clothes.

There are only about 1.5 million Jains in India today, but because they specialize in business and finance, their influence is out of proportion to their numbers. Their wealth enables them to maintain temple complexes unrivaled by any religious monuments in India.

The Jains have a rich tradition in art and temple architecture. Their sculptures are renowned for perfection and a quality of calm. The human images you will see are those of the twenty-four Tirthankaras said to have achieved enlightenment by conquering their worldly desires (the word "Jain" is derived from the Sanskrit for "conqueror"). Because their numbers are small (in an India of over 800 million people) the probability of finding them is greatly increased if you go to one of their temples.

## Sites—Jainism

*Palitana, Gujarat*—Shatrunjaya Hill, about a mile from this town, is the Jain's Mecca. The faithful make pilgrimages to the 863 temples on top of this often mist-shrouded mountain.

*Parasnath Hill, Bihar*—Just northwest of the town of Dhanbad is where twenty of the twenty-four Tirthankaras are said to have achieved nirvana. Of the Jain temples here, Bhomia Baba and Samosavan are the ones to see.

*Mount Abu, Rajasthan*—This solitary, 4,000-foot-high plateau as been the Holy Mountain of the Jains since the eleventh century. Most of the temples were built between the eleventh and thirteenth centuries. The unadorned exterior of the Vimala Sha Temple (dedicated to Rasabhanatha, the first Tirthankara) does not look inviting, but you will be amazed by the layer upon layer of white marble filigree inside. It is almost like being inside a crystalline snowflake. To the side of the Vimala Sha Temple is the small, austere Digambara Temple of the "sky-clad" sect of Jains. Inside, the swastika, symbolic of security, is a prominent motif. Mount Abu is accessible by road from Udaipur.

## Alexander—Europe's First Invasion of Asia

In 326 B.C., Alexander the Great of Macedonia marched into India after defeating the Persian Empire (which included the Indus Valley region). Alexander's war-weary troops persuaded him to turn back home before they got very far into India, and the door between East and West was quickly closed—but not before Europe's first invasion into the heart of Asia could have its effects. A sudden transformation in Indian sculpture of the time strongly suggests that the Persian sculptors who were left jobless by Alexander's destruction of their homeland found employment at the royal courts of India.

## India's Asoka—A Bad Guy Sees the Light

A power vacuum was left when the Persians were defeated. The nearby Mauryan Empire of India stepped in to fill the vacuum. When Asoka,

the grandson of the Mauryan dynasty's founder took over the throne, he proved to be an able executive and empire-builder. In an incredible arms buildup, Asoka amassed an army of 700,000 warriors, 10,000 chariots, and 9,000 long-range elephants. He used torture, a secret police organization, and the death penalty to keep his subjects in line. All this changed when Asoka invaded Kalinga (present-day Orissa) on the east coast of India. For the first time, Asoka decided to go along for the fun and got a firsthand look at the slaughter. Shocked, he immediately renounced further conquest, embraced Buddhism, ceased sport hunting, and erected a monument of apology to the Kalingans (which can be seen today at Dhauli, near Bhubaneswar in Orissa state).

Asoka did for Buddhism what Constantine did for the Catholic Church. He sent Buddhist missionaries as far west as Greece, south to Sri Lanka, and into Southeast Asia and China. He had 84,000 stupas raised to commemorate events in the Buddha's life. A few of the polished stone columns he raised still stand for you to see.

## Mauryan Art

The best Asokan edict column to see is the one at Lauriya Nandangarth near the Nepalese border. It is not known how they raised this forty-seven-ton sandstone column in 241 B.C. The sculptures (capitals) on top of these columns are symbols of Buddha's teachings but exhibit strong Persian influence. The Persian sculptors who Asoka employed also brought their Greek apprentices along. The sculptures unearthed at the site of Asoka's capital city bear a close resemblance to the Ionic capitals of Greece. Persian and Greek artisans forever changed Indian sculpture.

---

# Sites—Mauryan Dynasty

*Patna Museum at Patna*—One of the finest masterpieces of Mauryan sandstone sculpture, the Didarganji Yakshi—remarkable for its brilliant polish—is at Patna.

*Sarnath*—When you find the Lion capital in the Sarnath Museum here, you may feel as if you have seen it somewhere before. This capital (which once sat atop an Asokan pillar) was adopted by the Indian government as its national emblem and can be seen reproduced on many banknotes and postage stamps. Originally, the lions atop the capital supported a wheel that symbolized the Buddhist "Wheel of Righteousness." It was significant that the symbol of religious law was placed above the lions, which symbolize brute force. The politicians who adopted this national symbol seem to be ignorant of the symbolism inherent in this capital, which now has the lions above four smaller wheels at their feet.

---

# The Kushan Empire

Asoka's Mauryan Empire declined after his death in 232 B.C., and Bactrian invaders moved into north India to fill the vacuum. The Bactrians were Greek remnants of Alexander the Great's empire. After Alexander returned home, they had established the kingdom of Bactria in the area of present-day Iran. The Bactrians new territory included Gandhara (in Afghanistan and Pakistan) and the city of Mathura (India)—a fact of little political importance but of great cultural significance. Buddhism in the region was in the process of great change—a change that gave birth to the new Mahayana form of the faith.

A fusion of Greek and local cultures began under the Bactrians. The conquering Bactrian general and ruler converted to Buddhism, and the Bactrian Greeks were replaced by a people called Kushans (called "Yueh-chih" by the Chinese). Their leader, Kanishka, also converted to Buddhism.

The Kushans were rich. Their territory served as an entrepot for trade between Rome, India, and China. The trade routes not only enriched the kingdom but brought foreigners and foreign influence to Kushan. The Kushans traveled, too—in A.D. 99, Kushan envoys were received by the Roman emperor Trajan.

Part of the change in Mahayana Buddhist cosmology was that the Buddha became not just a revered teacher and director of the way to salvation but a god. Up to this point, the Buddha had always been represented symbolically; by a wheel, an umbrella, an empty throne, or footsteps. This would no longer do for a god—the church had to come up with an image of its deity. It turned to alien Hellenized (Greek-influenced) craftsmen to produce the icon. The Gandharan craftsmen naturally drew upon their past experience of sculpting flattering standing images of Roman emperors in the Graeco-Roman style the nobility was so fond of. The Buddha images the Gandharans developed exude dignity and holiness. Most were painted and much more vivid than we see them today.

---

## Sites—Kushan/Gandharan Art

*Central Museum in Lahore, Pakistan*—Some of the best examples of Gandharan sculpture are found in this small museum near Punjab University. Do not miss the very famous Fasting Buddha sculpture or the sculpted image of a helmeted Athena (or Roma).

*Smithsonian Institution, Freer Gallery of Art, Washington, D.C.* —Check out
the carved Gandharan reliefs depicting the life of the Buddha. The detailed
carvings of people in the frieze will give you an idea of what people looked like
in second-century-A.D. Gandhara.

*Taxila, Pakistan*—Here, just thirty kilometers northeast of Rawalpindi, lie the
ruins of an ancient city. Taxila was founded about 200 B.C. and later occupied
by the Bactrian Greeks and the the Kushans, who made it into a cultural center. The remains of brick buildings are strewn over a wide area. The museum
is quite good and requires several hours itself.

*Also*: Look for fine examples of Gandharan art at the Peshawar Museum in
Peshawar, Pakistan and at the Mathura Museum in Mathura, India.

---

## The Gupta Empire—India's Age of Creativity

The greatest outpouring of creativity in Indian history happened while
the Guptas ruled from A.D. 320-480. The Hindu epic, the *Mahabharata*, was completed; Buddhist art flourished and became standardized; the decimal system was developed; and medicine became a
science.

Chandragupta I founded the empire in north India, but it was his
poet-writer-musician son, Samudragupta, who made it the dominant
power in the subcontinent. Although Samudragupta was Hindu, the
Guptans patronized and strengthened Buddhism—exporting the Hinayana form (see "Buddhism") of the faith to Southeast Asia, where it
coexisted with the Hinduism exported earlier from India.

Guptan art is the classic art of India. Guptan Buddhist art is distinguished by the standardization of the images of a round-bodied Buddha in a sitting position. Literature did not suffer under the Guptans,
either. India's Shakespeare, Kalidasa, wrote the epic play *Shakuntala*
and the lyrical poem "Cloud Messenger" in the fifth century.

# Sites—Gupta Empire

*Ajanta caves*—Twenty-nine temples and monasteries are situated here, painstakingly cut into a rock gorge by Buddhist artisans. Famous for frescoes illustrating the flowering of Buddhist art. The first caves were started about 200 B.C. and the last ones finished about A.D. 650. Cave 19 exhibits the best in art and architecture of the Gupta period (A.D. 320-650). Seemingly every inch of this cave's wall surface is covered with carvings. Contrast the many post-A.D. 450 Mahayana images of the Buddha in Cave 19 with the strictly symbolic representation of him in the earlier Hinayana-period caves at Ajanta. Notice also that the stupa at the end of Cave 19 is more of a spire than the short dome stupas seen in the earlier caves (Cave 10) at Ajanta. The elongation and elaboration of the indoor stupas here parallels the transformation of the early Indian stupas into the tall pagodas of China.

*Archaeological Museum at Sarnath, India*—Although Asoka erected stupas here to commemorate the spot where the Buddha offered his first teachings, the work continued under the Gupta rulers, and this museum preserves some of their finest works.

# Classical China—The Shang and Chou

While the science of Harappan sewage engineering was at its apogee, the Chinese were just getting the prerequisites out of the way. The Chinese were slower starters, but it did not take them long to create Asia's other major civilization. Both Chinese legend and archaeological evidence point to the North China plain and Yellow River basin as the cultural homeland of the Chinese people. The first Chinese dynasty, the Hsia, remains legendary because archaeologists have not found any physical evidence of it yet. Early Chinese historical records date the Hsia dynasty from 2205 to 1766 B.C.

The Chinese have made matters easy for tourists by organizing their history into about (there is some disagreement in number) twenty-four dynasties. The dynasties came and went with rulers and centered around personalities. The Chinese, given the benefit of a couple of thousand years or so, noticed a pattern—a new dynasty would be founded by good men, the empire would grow and prosper and then decline, being pulled down by evil monarchs. Government expenses would grow, imperial prestige would suffer, territory would be lost and rebellions begun. A general or a nearby state would take over, name the new dynasty in their honor, and often move the capital.

The first dynasty from which artifacts have been found is the Shang (probably 1765-1123 B.C.). Chinese civilization remained at its origin on the north China plain during the Shang dynasty. Much of what is even today quintessentially Chinese had its origin in Shang dynasty China, including written characters (carved into animal bones and tortoise shells), woven silk, commodity merchants, ancestor worship, and taxes. The noblemen of the time liked to take all their toys with them to the grave. A tomb unearthed at Anyang had one dead nobleman in it, along with seventy-nine people (bodyguards, concubines, etc.), eleven dogs, twenty-seven horses, three monkeys, and one deer that had been killed and buried with him. Another nearby tomb had 12,000 people and animals buried with an apparently gregarious occupant.

The long-lived Chou (or "Zhou") dynasty (1027-256 B.C.) came next. There were many wars and much strife during this period. The king ran his domain through delegated lords who controlled assigned areas. Eventually the fighting between these fiefdoms ended the Chou, when one state—the Ch'in—triumphed. The Chou dynasty was not a total cultural loss, however—the political chaos bred intellectual creativity, and feudal lords gathered philosophers around them.

## Chinese Bronzes and Bones

The most tangible remains of Shang times in China are the superb bronze vessels and the animal bones used for divination. At about the time the Druids were raising the stones at Stonehenge, the Chinese were producing bronze works of art that have never been surpassed.

The Bronze Age seems to have occurred independently in several places on earth, including the central plains of China's Yellow River Valley. Unlike their fellow Bronze Age earthlings, the Chinese metallurgists made food and wine vessels for royalty rather than weapons for soldiers. These works of art bestowed power upon their owners, and only rulers could possess them (it took armies of costly artisans to cast the bronzes). When power changed hands, so did the bronzes.

A majority of the bronzes you are likely to see in museums (there are about 12,000 bronzes in collections) will be identified as wine or food vessels. The Shang rulers liked their wine, as did the royal ancestors. Frequent offerings of wine were presented to the ancestors and deities, who consumed the spirit of the wine but left the liquid for the mortals to finish off. The Shang became more devoted to their wine than to their ancestors, and drunkenness became such a problem in high places that the Chou cited it as a reason for their usurpation of the Shang rule.

Look closely at the detailed design on the Shang bronzes, and you are likely to find the t'ao t'ieh ("glutton mask")—the most popular Shang decoration. The mask is formed by two confronting, stylized animals with snouts, horns, legs, and tails. The t'ao t'ieh must have been a potent symbol, but scholars today can not agree on what, if anything, it symbolized.

The bronzes we see in the museum today do not look like the lustrous golden vessels that were put before the ancestors in rituals. We have these artifacts to look at because they were either buried by people fleeing invaders or were buried with the royal deceased. For centuries the buried vessels were oxidized by salts in the earth, and when finally found, they look like rusty blobs of iron. After cleaning, a beautiful patina of blues and greens, unintended by the artists, covers the bronze.

The Chou people who defeated the Shang were a vigorous people out of the west. As wise conquerors, the Chou absorbed Shang culture rather than destroy it. Excellent bronzes continued to roll out of the royal foundries, but changes in design reflected a change in society. The Shang agricultural-hunting culture was replaced by the Chou's urban and feudal agricultural system. Bronzes of the period show a decline in lively animistic themes. Chou bronzes began to carry long inscriptions, usually lauding the achievements of their commissioner/owner.

China's earliest written records were found in a pile of Shang-era bones. In 1899 archaeologists were distraught to find that animal bones bearing primitive Chinese character-writing from Shang times were being ground up and used for medicine by Chinese apothecaries. The source of the bones, near Peking, had been used by the druggists for decades, maybe centuries, before the looting was stopped. The bones that are left tell of important national events and about daily life of the Shang royal family.

The Shang rulers used these bones to divine the future. Specialists burned or bored holes in the bones to cause cracking and then foretold the future by "reading" the cracks. The questions, answers, and events were then inscribed on the bones using the earliest forms of Chinese ideographs.

## Sites—Shang Dynasty

*Anyang in Henan Province*—The site of the Shang capital. It was not until a treasure trove of inscribed bronze vessels was dug up here in 1934 that Western archaeologists could believe the artifacts were made 3,000 years ago. At the site are remains of fifty-six buildings and several tombs. You may sometimes see this site referred to as the "Yin Ruins," because the Chou referred to their Shang predecessors as the "Yin."

*National Palace Museum in Taipei, Taiwan*—Probably the world's best collection of Shang bronzes (over 4,000 pieces) and oracle bones. Exhibits are very well explained and presented.

*Metropolitan Museum in New York City*—The new Weber Gallery for the arts of ancient China at the Metropolitan presents Chinese art from Neolithic to T'ang times. Be sure to see the "Tuan-fang" altar set—it is a complete kit, including matching food and wine vessels and a bronze altar table. It was unearthed in Shansi Province in 1901 and named after the Manchu viceroy who owned it until it was sold to the museum in 1924. Also in North America, check out the Nelson Art Gallery-Atkins Museum in Kansas City and the Royal Ontario Museum in Canada.

# Confucius (to Avoid Confucian)

While Siddhartha Gautama (the Buddha) was searching for enlightenment under the bodhi tree in India, his contemporary in China, K'ung Fu-tzu (Confucius), was shuffling around north China, trying to get one of the Chou lords to listen to his program.

Probably the most misspelled philosophy of all time, Confucianism is not even a word in Chinese. It is not a religion, either. It is the reformist philosophy espoused by a remarkable civil servant who felt that the world was quite out of joint. He taught that anyone might become noble through just and kind behavior, and he dismissed the aristocrats' claim that nobility was something one had to be born into.

IMAGE OF CONFUCIUS.

Confucius taught his philosophy to poor and rich students alike. He considered it wrong to become either a recluse or to simply "follow the crowd." Although he felt convention was the cement of society, he sought to change conventions he thought harmful or immoral. His objective was happiness for people in the here-and-now, and since happiness could be achieved only if everyone exhibited correct behavior, he wrote a how-to guide called the *Analects*. Here Confucius laid down his observations and analysis of correct behavior. He prescribed rules in detail and stressed that he did not know the "Truth" but only the way to look for it.

Many of his students passed the civil service tests and took jobs in government. As they rose in the hierarchy, they began to exert influence and incorporate Confucius' teachings into government policies. Confucius did not live long enough to see significant change, however, and in 479 B.C. he died, thinking himself a failure. His teachings lived through his disciples and writings, though, and later they gained popularity. The Chinese bureaucracy gave a new meaning to "posthumous honors" by waiting twelve-hundred years to award Confucius with the title of "Prince of Literary Enlightenment." Today, much of Chinese, Korean, and Japanese ethics is of Confucian derivation.

Confucius, the man, was born ten miles east of Qufu in the village of Nisan in Shandong Province. In Confucius' day, however, there was no Shandong Province—or any other of today's provinces. At this time China was divided into many small principalities, and present-day Shandong encompasses the territory of four of these old states. Confucius owed his allegiance to his home state of Lu—and in fact served as Lu's acting minister of state for a while before hitting the road in vain search of a moral prince who would hire him.

The influence of Confucius's thought would have to wait until later, however, as the proponents of a completely opposite philosophy came to power with the Ch'in killing of the last Chou ruler in 249 B.C.

---

# Sites—Confucius

*Temple and Home of Confucius at Qufu in Shandong Province*—The three rooms of Confucius's home were turned into a temple the year after his death in 479 B.C., and annual sacrifices in his honor have taken place here ever since. Subsequent emperors enlarged the grounds and built new tributes to the sage, so that this is one of the best locations to view the development of traditional architecture. The Pavilion of the Constellation of Scholars, begun in the Sung dynasty, is one of the finest wooden pagodas in China. Bronze vessels from the Shang dynasty, rare woodblocks from the Sung and Yuan dynasties, and an exhibit of garments from the Yuan, Ming, and Qing dynasties are in the Mansion of Confucius. All that is left of his home, however, is a well. Go to nearby Yanzhou by train from Peking and take a bus on to Qufu.

P.S. The birthplace of Mencius (Meng Tse), the chief successor to Confucius and considered China's second-ranking philosopher, is at Zouxian, only twenty-five miles south of Qufu.

---

It is interesting to note the difference between the philosophers of the two great civilizations of Asia. While Indic thinkers concerned themselves with metaphysics, the Chinese stressed political thought and devised moral codes for improving the here-and-now.

## The Ch'in—China's First Empire

The Ch'in (or "Qin") dynasty was a one-man show. Chin Shih Huang Ti (also spelled Qin Shihuangdi) unified China and established an imperial system guided by the forceful measures espoused by the legalist school of philosophers. Any action to maintain the ruler's power was justified. The ruler was all-wise and could not be questioned. Chin Shih Huang Ti may have been all-wise, but he also became one of the most hated emperors in history. He spent much of his time looking for the secret of eternal life, enslaving thousands to build the Great Wall, and paying his soldiers on a commission basis for each enemy head brought in. They brought in as many as 400,000 heads at a time.

Westerners derived the name "China" from "Ch'in." The Chinese call their country Zhongguo (Middle Kingdom).

GREAT WALL OF CHINA.

# Sites—Ch'in Dynasty

*Xian in Shaanxi Province*—Thirty kilometers east of Xi'an lies the mausoleum and buried pottery army of Chin Shih Huang Ti. The mausoleum is a seventy-six-meter-high (after 2,200 years of erosion, mind you) mound of rammed earth. Just to the east of the mound, a 230-meter-long pit containing 6,000 life-size terra-cotta (waterproof ceramic clay) soldiers, horses, and chariots was found in the 1970s. Now excavated, the sight of the pottery army, which was meant to protect the emperor in his afterlife, is something you will remember for a long time.

*The Ling Canal in Guangxi Province*—Chin Shih Huang Ti had this thirty-four-kilometer-long canal dug in 214 B.C. to link the Xiang and Li rivers and make north-south travel easy. The Qin Dyke lies at the most scenic portion of the canal. You can get to the canal by train from Guilin, sixty-six kilometers to the south.

---

## Han Dynasty—China Expands Westward

The Ch'in dynasty fell to Liu Pang, a military adventurer, just three years after Chin Shih Huang Ti's death. Liu was the first in a long line of Han emperors over the 400 years of the dynasty. China was greatly expanded by the Han—adding the area of Gansu and Turkestan as well as establishing dominion over Tonkin (Vietnam) and Korea.

After the Chinese claimed the far west (Central Asia), Buddhist missionaries from India and Afghanistan moved into the pacified area to spread the faith. During the first century A.D., Buddhism made its way into the Han capital of Chang'an (present-day Xi'an) from the Central Asian outpost.

---

## Sites—Han Dynasty

*Xi'an*—Site of the capital in Han and T'ang times. The Xianyang Museum in the city has an extensive collection of Han dynasty artifacts. The mound tomb of Han emperor Wu Ti (Liu Che), fifty kilometers west of Xi'an, is the largest of eleven Han imperial tombs. Do not miss the sculpture of the Han horse trampling a Hsiung Nu (Hun) soldier.

---

When the Han fell in A.D. 220, China slipped into three and a half centuries of political turmoil and feudalism. Things were a mess, but Chinese historians (who like to tidy things up) decided to call this period the Six Dynasties, after they weeded out the superfluous states.

## Sri Lanka—Asoka's Son Brings Buddhism

India's Asoka had sent his son to the island of Ceylon in the third century B.C. to spread Buddhist teachings. The orthodox Theravada Buddhism he successfully transplanted to the island has survived to become the primary influence in the lives of most of the native Sinhalese people today.

Hindu Tamils from southern India later flowed into Ceylon, and today 26 percent of the people in Sri Lanka are ethnic Tamils. In recent years friction between the Sinhalese and Tamil peoples of Sri Lanka has escalated into violence. At the time of this writing, Indian troops were in Sri Lanka by invitation to act as a peace-keeping force in the Tamil-dominated north of the island.

## Funan—Southeast Asia's First Empire

Southeast Asia's first great empire began in what is now Kampuchea (Cambodia) in the first century A.D. Within two centuries Funan controlled all of today's Kampuchea and parts of Vietnam, Thailand, and Malaysia. Chinese travelers described the Khmer people of Funan as frizzy-haired and black.

Although originally a Buddhist state, the Hindu cult of Siva became the state religion of Funan in the fifth century. The Gupta Empire in India established contact with Funan and the rest of Southeast Asia at this time and the process of Indianization quickened.

In the sixth century, Funan faded as other Khmer people from Laos moved in to replace Funan with the state of Chenla. Chenla lasted for about 250 years and was in turn absorbed by the Khmer kingdom of Kambuja. Only small figurines in the Indian Gupta style remain as reminders of Funan. No buildings or temples have survived.

## The Koreans

The Koreans found their peninsula early (about 2000 B.C.) and stuck with it. Although China and Japan each invaded or occupied the coun-

COREAN EGG-SELLER.—*Native Drawing.*

try three times, the Koreans held their ground (there was nowhere else to go in their little cul-de-sac of a peninsula), and today Korea is nearly 100 percent ethnic Korean.

The first Koreans probably came from north of China. The Korean language is very different from Chinese but has much in common with a family of languages (including Mongolian and Turkish) that originated in Mongolia.

Despite the people's non-Chinese origin, Korean society has more than a teacup of Chinese culture. Around 100 B.C., during the first Chinese occupation of northern Korea, the Chinese set up a commandery near present-day Pyongyang (capital of North Korea). When the Han dynasty fell in China, the Korean kingdom of Koguryo swallowed the Chinese commandery and quite a bit of Chinese culture along with it. During the fourth century A.D., Confucianism, Buddhism, and Chinese political structure were introduced to Koguryo.

# Japan—Before the Japanese

Just as North America has its native American people, Japan has its native Japanese. The Ainu, a hairy and "round-eyed" people, were probably original inhabitants of the islands, but like the native Americans, the Ainu were pushed back by a new people. The difference is that the newcomers in Japan arrived more than 2,000 years ago.

The Japanese are of mixed origin. Their language and archaelogical remains point to Northeast Asia, but some linguistic evidence also points to a Southeast Asian strain. The Japanese, like Southeast Asians, are generally smaller and darker than Northeast Asians. Ethnographers also believe that early mixing with the Ainu is the reason Japanese usually have more facial hair than other Asians.

The people we now think of as Japanese were a confederation of 100 tribes on Kyushu Island when Chinese writers described them around the third century A.D. The Chinese said the "Great Wa" ("Wa" may have meant "dwarf") or Yamato (Mountain-East) peoples liked to drink, fish, and weave. Tattoos indicated which social class a person belonged to.

By the fourth century A.D., the Japanese had expanded out of Kyushu onto the large island of Honshu and even onto the Korean peninsula, where they formed the small state of Kaya. There were many early ties between the Koreans and Japanese. There is some speculation that the rulers in Kyushu had come from Korea in the first centuries A.D. By the ninth century fully a third of all families of the nobility had a foreign (mostly Korean) origin.

Japan's imperial family of today is directly descended from the Yamato rulers of the fifth century. Unlike anywhere else in the world, there has not been a break in the Japanese ruling line in at least fifteen centuries. This direct connection with the hazy origins of their culture explains the special relationship the Japanese have with their emperors.

(KIKU-NO-MON)

**Japanese Imperial Crest—the Chrysanthemum**

# Sites—Early Japan

*Tokyo National Museum*—This is the best collection of Japanese art and artifacts in the world. More than 86,000 items are housed here, including some from Korea and China. Located in Tokyo's scenic Ueno Park. Closed Mondays.

*Beppu University Ancient Culture Museum*—In the city of Beppu on Kyushu Island, where Japanese civilization began. A good collection of archaeological artifacts from the Jomon (10,000-250 B.C.), Yayoi (250 B.C.-A.D. 250) and Yamato (A.D. 250-552) periods. Note that the Yamato period is often referred to as the "Kofun" period, because members of the Yamato ruling class were buried in keyhole-shaped mounds called "kofun."

## Meanwhile. . . Events Outside Asia

### Harappan civilization and Shang dynasty: 2500-1000 B.C.
—Cretans learn how to make bronze (ca. 3000 B.C.)
—Pyramids at Giza built (ca. 2500 B.C.)
—Fall of Troy to the Greeks (ca. 1150 B.C.)

### Chou dynasty: 1027-221 B.C.
—Parthenon completed during Golden Age of Athens (ca. 450 B.C.)
—Alexander the Great's empire stretches from Greece to India (323 B.C.)
—Roman Republic founded (ca. 500 B.C.)
—Ptolemy is governor of Egypt (323 B.C.)

### Early Indian Kingdoms (Mauryan, Andhra, Gupta): 322 B.C.-A.D. 480
—Hannibal commits suicide to avoid capture by Romans (183 B.C.)
—Julius Caesar and Cleopatra hit it off (47 B.C.)
—Romans take Britain (A.D. 77)
—Goths sack Athens (A.D. 268)
—Attila the Hun invades Italy (A.D. 452)
—Roman Empire falls (A.D. 476)

# 6

# The Golden Age (A.D. 500-1500)

The millennium between A.D. 500 and 1500 could be called the Golden Age of Asian civilization. While Europe sank into the Dark Ages, much of Asia experienced a cultural renaissance. The weight of world civilization seemed to tilt to the East—even the Roman Empire shifted its center east to Constantinople (Istanbul), where Europe and Asia stare at one another across less than a mile of water.

The great Asian cities of Angkor, Pagan, Ayuthia, Chang'an, and Kyongju flourished, declined, and then were abandoned by their creators. Travelers today can visit the ruins of these great cities that once outclassed their European contemporaries. Ambivalent feelings of sadness and awe may wash over even the most detached visitor seeing any of these ruins for the first time. Understanding their stories will make the ruins come alive.

## China—The Empire Strikes Back

After the collapse of the Han dynasty in A.D. 220, China slipped into four centuries of political turmoil and division (the Six Dynasties era).

Like India, China was divided into a number of relatively short-lived kingdoms of limited geographic scope until the Sui dynasty reunited the nation in A.D. 589. The Sui dynasty lasted only twenty-nine years, but it was enough time to restore law and order, reintegrate parts of Central Asia into the empire, and extend public works. Bungled Chinese efforts to invade Korea sparked revolts and brought down the Sui. The rebel leader Li Yuan founded the great T'ang (rhymes with "song") dynasty in A.D. 618 and ushered in China's most brilliant epoch.

## T'ang China

Scarcely a hundred years after the sacking of Rome, the Chinese reveled in their most brilliant dynasty—the T'ang. If asked, nine out of ten modern Chinese probably would say they prefer T'ang as the dynasty of choice.

At a time when Europe suffered racial and religious conflict, T'ang China welcomed Syrians, Greeks, Armenians, Japanese, and others who flocked to China to trade wares and products. Many of the aliens chose to stay and live among the Chinese. Chang'an, the T'ang capital, became one of the world's most cosmopolitan cities.

These were times of cruelty and bloodshed as well. The much-hated Empress Wu maneuvered her way into control by framing the previous empress and another rival, having their hands and feet cut off and enjoying a good chuckle while she watched them slowly die. Only eight out of eighteen T'ang emperors died a natural death—the rest were murdered. The favored way to dispatch an unwanted emperor was to slip him a tall glass of powdered jade.

The T'ang was also the Golden Age of Chinese literature. The spirit of T'ang was expressed in a flurry of poetic work. While potters excelled at recreating animal forms, the T'ang poets were inspired by natural landscapes. It is no coincidence that the most revered T'ang poets came from the lofty mountains and stimulating scenery of Sichuan (Szechwan) Province.

The Chinese began using the potter's wheel 1,000 years after it was first used in West Asia, but T'ang potters excelled at its use soon after they figured out a way to fire the pottery at higher temperatures to make harder pots.

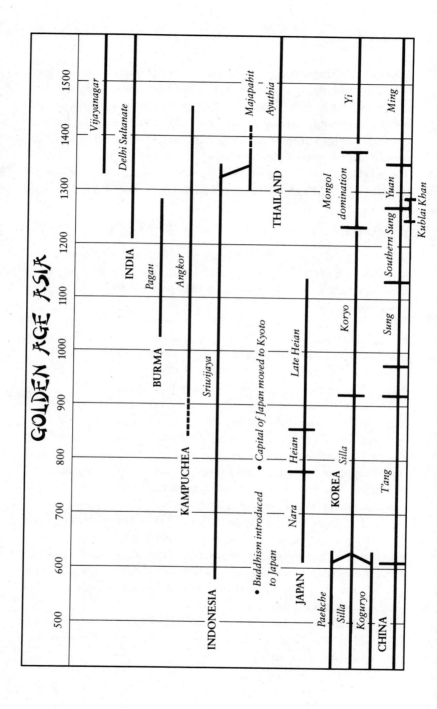

The T'ang Chinese love for animals, especially horses, is reflected in the abundance of animal figurines that have been found. If any one object epitomizes the T'ang it must be the ceramic horse. Irregularly splashed with the T'ang artisan's favorite yellow, brown, and green glazes, the T'ang horses exhibit the arched neck of the Arabian horses that emperors received as tribute from Central Asian tribes. Many—if not most—of the T'ang horses and pottery around today came from graves dug up in the early twentieth century.

The accomplishments of the T'ang artisans would not be so widely known to us today if the Chinese of the period had not had the custom of burying their relatives with little figurines that did not decay. People were buried with token horses, attendants, musicians, dishware, and of course, concubines for the dead men. Tossing objets d'art into the graves developed into such an extravagance, as the bereaved sought to outdo the bereaved of other families, that the government had to limit the number of objects sent down with grandfather. In later times, to the chagrin of art collectors today, the Chinese opted to send off their loved ones by burning paper models of the deceased's possessions at the grave site.

## Sung China—Zenith of Chinese Culture and Art

The T'ang dynasty of China fell to a rebellion in A.D. 906, and China drifted in confusion for over half a century until the Sung united most of the country. Although the Sung never reestablished the firm central-ized administration of T'ang, Chinese culture and arts reached their zenith during the Sung and subsequent Southern Sung. Japanese art of this period (late Heian in Japan) borrowed heavily from China.

The art of the Sung was more restrained than the exuberance of the T'ang. Ceramics made during Sung times emphasize form over decor-ation—in contrast to the highly decorated ceramics of the T'ang arti-sans. Sung potters experimented with firing techniques and mater-ials—developing celadon, a green-gray ware, often purposely crackled, that has been highly prized by collectors since. Celadon was further perfected by Korean artisans who were in contact with the Chinese.

# Sites—Golden Age of China

*Mogao Caves at Dunhuang in Gansu Province*—It is well worth a trip into far western Gansu Province to see the beginnings of Buddhist art in China and the works of a subsequent millennium. Here you can follow the progression of Buddhist art from the heavily Indian-influenced times of the Northern Wei dynasty to the Sinicized and lifelike forms of the T'ang dynasty. A cache of very rare T'ang paintings on silk was found here in the first decade of the twentieth century, and many made their way to the British Museum in London, where they can be seen today.

*Maijishan Caves, forty-five kilometers southeast of Tianshui in Gansu Province*—So many caves are carved into the cliff of this mountain that it looks like a honeycomb. Buddhist artisans started chiseling away at Maiji Mountain in A.D. 384 and continued for over fifteen-hundred years. The fifteen-meter-high Sui dynasty Buddha in Cave 13 is the largest image at Maijishan.

*Longmen Caves, twelve kilometers south of Luoyang in Henan Province*—Some of the best examples of the Buddhist art of Northern Wei and T'ang dynasties can be seen here. There is plenty to see—97,000 statues, 1,352 caves, and forty pagodas. The serenity and power evident in the face of the seventeen-meter-high Buddha in the Fengxian Temple is characteristic of T'ang Buddhist images.

*Yungang Caves, fifteen kilometers west of Datong in Shanxi Province*—Fifty-three Buddhist caves were carved into a one-kilometer-long cliff over the course of several dynasties, beginning in A.D. 453. Lively relief carvings of tales of the Buddha's life in Cave 6 are some of the best work among the 51,000 carved images at Yungang. The richness of detail and realism in the carving of the Buddhist pantheon here makes this the best of China's Buddhist cave complexes.

*Bingling Monastery Caves in Gansu Province*—About two-thirds of the sculptures carved into the red cliffs are works of T'ang craftsmen. The largest, one of a seated Buddha, is over thirty meters tall. Cave 169 is from Western Qin times (A.D. 420), and the oldest known cave inscription in China is on the wall here.

*Xi'an*—Called Chang'an during T'ang times, this city was the center of China at her most brilliant moment. The Great Mosque here was built in A.D. 742 and clearly shows a Sinification of Islamic architecture. The minaret looks like a pagoda.

---

## The Mongol Invasion

The Sung dynasty was not pulled down from within by revolt but overthrown from without by the Mongols of Kublai Khan. China had suffered at the hands of nomadic tribes at her flanks before, but for the first time, China was totally defeated by an invader.

The Mongol's defeat of Sung China and territories to the west once again brought China into contact with the Middle East and Europe. A single family—the house of Genghis Khan—conquered half the known world, from Korea to Turkey. Genghis Khan's Mongol Empire was the largest empire the world has seen.

As north China disentegrated into political chaos following the T'ang dynasty, the tribes north of the Great Wall fought among themselves, with first the Khitans and then the Jurchen (from Manchuria) gaining control of the area between Mongolia and the Yellow Sea. South China was spared the turmoils of the north, and by A.D. 960 had united under the Sung dynasty.

While the Sung and the subsequent Southern Sung dynasties coasted in a sea of tranquillity and refined civilization for a couple of centuries, the Mongols in the far north used horses to expand their empire as far west as southern Russia. Their leader was Temuchin, who, along with his brothers, had been kicked out of the clan when his father died. He fought his way to the top of the Mongol world, took the name of Genghis Khan (Ruler of the Universe) and set out to prove his name.

When Genghis died in 1227 he had not quite conquered the universe, but he had made life miserable for Koreans, Persians, Russians, and everyone else in his vast empire. Genghis' descendants maintained and expanded the empire, carrying out raids as far into Europe as Budapest (Hungary) and present-day Poland.

The southern Chinese proved to be the Mongols' most stubborn would-be victims. It was not until Genghis' grandson, Kublai Khan, took the Sung capital of Hangzhou in 1276 that Chinese resistance crumbled.

Kublai became not only the ruler of the Mongol Empire but the emperor of China as well, taking the name of Yuan (original) for his dynasty. He became a good Chinese. He took up ancestor worship, encouraged Chinese arts, moved his capital from Mongolia to China (to the site of present-day Peking), and instituted many projects designed to make the commoners' lives easier.

Kublai altered the course of the Yellow River and built canals for transport, established an empire-wide version of the Pony Express, and added Yunnan Province to the Chinese Empire. The consolidation of the Empire once more made trade routes to Europe passable, and the imperial highway system was thronged with travelers, traders, and diplomats. China and Europe were no longer strangers, thanks to the Mongols.

## The Polos—Merchants of Venice

One family that did not wait for the roads to be improved were the Polos of Venice (Italy). Seventeen-year-old Marco Polo, his father and uncle set out for China in 1271 on a trading venture. The two elders had been to Kublai Khan's new capital at Dadu the previous decade and had been sent back to Europe with a request for 100 Christian missionaries from the Pope. Two unenthusiatic Dominican friars and some holy oil from the sepulcher of Christ at Jerusalem started out on the return journey to China with the Polos. The oil and the Polos made it to Kublai's pleasure palace at Shangtu (called Xanadu in Coleridge's famous poem) but the friars had turned back at the first sign of discomfort.

The Polos stayed in China for seventeen years, living in Dadu (Peking) and Yangchow (near Hangzhou). Marco was the only Polo to record some of his experiences in China (a few years after his return to Venice). Marco was a merchant, not a writer / adventurer, and his lifeless reminiscences leave huge.gaps in the Polo story. Marco had a lot to say about Kublai Khan and Peking, but he never mentioned the Great Wall, the then-popular custom of binding women's feet, tea (unknown in Europe at the time), sulphur matches, or the compass ( both also unknown in Europe).

Kublai Khan died while the Polos were en route back to Venice. Kublai's Mongol successors succumbed to the good life during the next century and deteriorated into powerless figures behind palace walls. The Chinese, led by secret societies, took China back in 1368 and founded the Ming (bright) dynasty. The Mongol Empire was gone, but its traces live on.

---

# Sites—Mongols

*Mausoleum of Genghis Khan*—At Atengxilian in China's Inner Mongolia. When Genghis died in 1227, he was taken back to the Erduosi Plateau and buried here according to his wishes. The Mongolian tent-shaped mausoleum shelters the bier of the Khan and his three wives.

---

## Chinese Civilization Comes to Korea and Japan

During the first century A.D., two less Sinicized Korean kingdoms had arisen south of the Koguryo Kingdom we discussed in chapter 5, Ancient Asia. The location of these two kingdoms roughly approximates the part of the Korean Peninsula where South Korea is now. Paekche ruled the area where Seoul is today, and the Silla arose in the southeast corner of the peninsula. In the seventh century A.D., Silla, with the help of the T'ang Chinese, defeated Paekche and Koguryo and unified Korea for the first time. Korean unity lasted until the twentieth-century Japanese occupation and the subsequent division into North and South Korea in our century.

Along with T'ang help in crushing Silla's Korean rivals came T'ang influence and Chinese culture. Even before the T'ang, Buddhism and Chinese writing were brought to Korea and adopted. Chinese culture passed through Korea to Japan as well, brought by traveling Buddhist monks. The Japanese adopted Chinese-style administration and built

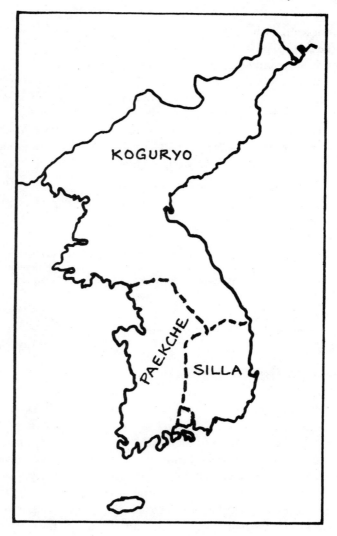

a new capital at Nara and then at Kyoto, laid out to replicate the T'ang capital of Chang'an (see Kyoto).

We get the word "Korea" from the Koryo Kingdom, which replaced Silla in the tenth century. The North Koreans call their country "Choson" (Land of Morning Calm) and the South Koreans use the ancient name "Hanguk" (Land of the Han People).

# Sites—Silla Kingdom

*Kyongju, South Korea*—This is the ancient city of Korea. Not on the mammoth scale of Angkor (Kampuchea) or as otherworldly as Ayuthia (Thailand), Kyongju nonetheless exudes an aura of learned contemplation. The capital of the Silla Kingdom for almost a thousand years, Kyongju has 2,000-year-old royal tombs, palaces, an astronomical observatory, temples, and beautiful scenery. The mountains surrounding the area are filled with pagodas, temples, and statues. The National Museum here is even better than the National Museum in Seoul. Do not miss Pulguksa Temple or Sokkuram Grotto—but be prepared for masses of people. Kwaenung Tomb is a nice place to get away from the crowds.

For beautiful relief carvings, visit Okryongsa Temple in Kyongju's Pagoda Valley.

# Japan's Golden Age

The traveler in search of old Japan will need to leave the capital city of Tokyo and head southwest to the cities of Nara and Kyoto. From the seventh to the twelfth centuries, the Imperial throne rested here in what the Japanese call the Kinki District. It was here that Japanese culture blossomed. Logically enough, the 184 years (600-784) that the capital lay at Nara is known as the Nara period. The museum-goer will need to know, however, that the subsequent four centuries after the capital was moved to Kyoto are known as the Heian period, because the original name of the area was Heian Kyo, or "Peace and Ease Capital." The name was later changed to Kyoto (Western Capital).

While the Imperial court resided at Nara, Buddhism was accepted as the state religion, and some of the greatest Buddhist temples of Asia were constructed in the city. Horyuji and Todaiji Temples were initiated. The emperor and his court began to devote much of their time to the study of Buddhism and the arts. The aristocrat's devotion to the arts and religion continued after the court moved to Kyoto. China was looked to as a model and source of artistic inspiration (both Nara and Kyoto were laid out to resemble the Chinese capital of Chang'an), but Japanese artisans gradually began to assert a uniquely Japanese style.

The Imperial court became increasingly interested in the arts and court etiquette and less and less interested in running the country. While Lady Murasaki Shikibu of the Imperial court wrote Asia's first historical novel, *The Tale of Genji*, the Fujiwara family assumed the court's political and military responsibilities. The emperors continued to be venerated as religious leaders of the nation, but the Fujiwara and their friends exercised real control.

The ground was laid during this period for the coming Feudal Age of Japan. An increasing number of local nobles were given tax-free status. Heavily taxed landowners began to place their property in the hands of the tax-free aristocracy to avoid taxes while retaining the right to live on and work the land. The land holdings of nobles thus grew— along with their power. Central authority was further eroded as scattered tax-free "kingdoms" became autonomous.

## Korean and Japanese Writing

Both the early Koreans and Japanese had their own distinct spoken languages—but neither had a writing system. During the Silla times in Korea, scholars learned Chinese and composed poetry and kept records in the foreign language. In the seventh century A.D., a way was devised to use the Chinese characters to phonetically represent the Korean language.

Chinese characters are ideographs, symbols representing a thing or idea rather than a sound. Thus Koreans and Japanese could use the Chinese character representing a cat, but pronounce the word for cat in their own native language. You can pick up today's newspaper in China, Korea, or Japan and see this combination of two characters used to write the word for "China":

中國

In China, these characters are pronounced "Zhongguo," in Korea it is "Chungguk," and in Japan it would be read as "Chugoku."

Although the Japanese invented their own phonetic writing system in the ninth century, and Korea's King Sejong invented an easy-to-learn syllabary (hangul) in the fifteenth century, both nations continue to mix these phonetic syllabaries with Chinese characters in the same sentence. Characters continue to be necessary because of the many homophones (words that sound alike) in these three languages. If purely phonetic writing systems were used, too many words would be spelled exactly alike.

The sound "jian" in Chinese can mean any of the following:

见          舰          荐          监          鉴
to see      warship     to introduce  a eunuch    mirror

闰          剑          谏          煎          贱
opening     sword       to advise    to boil      cheap

Unlike the tonal, monosyllabic language of the Chinese, Korean and Japanese are toneless polysyllabic languages.

How to say "thanks"

| Chinese Mandarin | Xie xie | two syllables |
| Korean | Kamsahamnida | five syllables |
| Japanese | Arigato gozaimasu | eight syllables |

## Southeast Asia—Great Kingdoms Emerge

The Burmans, the Thai, and the Vietnamese who had moved south out of China into Southeast Asia became good farmers and seamen. The Mekong River Valley was perfect for rice farming, and coastal waters provided them with both food and a means of easy international travel for trade purposes. Powerful kingdoms began to emerge about A.D. 600, and in the coming centuries the states of modern Asia would begin to take form. But in 1500, there was no "Thailand," no "Indonesia," no "Vietnam."

## The Thai—Sideline Survivors

The Thai people have not always lived in Thailand. They started out in what is Yunnan Province in China, where they founded the kingdom of Nanchao in the seventh century. Nanchao was crushed by the Mongols in 1253, but many Thai people had already moved south in previous centuries to what is northern Thailand today. The Thai newcomers drove the Khmers (Cambodians) out of northern Thailand and set up the vigorous but short-lived Kingdom of Sukhothai (1253-1378). That is where they were when the Mongols swept out of the north and did the Thai a favor by crushing the Burmans.

The Mongols invaded Burma and Indochina in 1282, overthrowing the great Kingdom of Pagan in Burma. It was more of a hit-and-run than an invasion, however. The Mongols from the north did not care much for the humidity and disease, the elephant-equipped armies of the southerners—or possibly they disliked the overwhelming, rotten smell of the local durian fruit. The Mongol conquerors turned toward home, leaving a power vacuum in the wake of their destruction and

withdrawal. Like all great power vacuums in history, this one was filled by sideline survivors—in this case, the neighboring Thai.

The subsequent Thai kingdom of Ayuthia was not only the most powerful Southeast Asian state of its time but the founder had the good sense to locate his great capital within a 20-baht (eighty-cent) bus ride from the Northern Bus Terminal in Bangkok. From 1350 to 1767 (when the Burmans destroyed it), this was the capital of the Thai kings. The kings taxed the people to pay for an incredible building spree of temples and palaces that rivaled any European city of the day. Today Europeans, among others, battle for taxis in the streets of nearby modern Ayuthia (pop. 52,000). The only modern amenities at ancient Ayuthia are two Chinese hotels and a floating restaurant or two.

Three hundred years ago, Europeans had their own little Eurotown in the kingdom's capital—the Chinese and the Japanese also had their own neighborhoods. During the latter part of the seventeenth century, a former Greek cabin boy named Constantine Phaulkon arrived in Ayuthia and bribed his way into a position of influence as an adviser to

RUINS OF A PAGODA AT AYUTHIA.

the king. The Thai king took a liking to Phaulkon, and by the time the Greek was forty years old he was the most powerful man in Thailand. It did not last. The Thais revolted against foreign influence in 1688, drove most Europeans out of the country and beheaded Phaulkon.

Ayuthia was situated on an island in the middle of the Chao Phraya River. The island was enclosed within walls that protected the capital against enemies. The brick-paved streets were wide and straight and lined with trees.

Thailand, like the other nations of Southeast Asia, has expanded and contracted over the years. During the Ayuthia period, the Thai kingdom extended from peninsular Malaya in the south to present-day Kampuchea in the east. The Thais were constantly at war with their neighbors, and their fortunes waxed and waned accordingly. In 1130 all of modern Thailand was under Khmer (Cambodian) control, but by 1352 the Thai had turned the tables and sacked the Khmer capital of Angkor. They did it again in 1393 for good measure. The Burmans recovered from their thirteenth-century whipping at the hands of the Mongols to sack and destroy Ayuthia in the eigthteenth century.

The Khmer thought of the king as a divine go-between with the gods. Before contact with the Khmers, the Thai kings had been accessible to any common man who rang the bell at the palace gate. After Khmerization the kings of Ayuthia became remote and unavailable.

As we will see, a combination of the Thais and large expenditures on monumental art projects led to the great Khmer fizzle. Ironically, these two influences converged—the Thais loved the art of the Khmers, and they appropriated it and changed it. The Thais did to Khmer art what the Romans had done to Greek art. Khmer art was classical, superior, and sophisticated. The Thais popularized it.

---

## Sites—The Thai

*Taihe in China's Yunnan Province*—All that is left of the eighth century capital of the Thai state of Nanchao are some foundations and two town walls made of rammed earth. A tablet found here records the wars fought between the Nanchao and T'ang China. The ruins are about seven kilometers from the picturesque town of Dali. The eleven-hour bus ride from Kunming to Dali will take you along the route of the Burma Road of World War II fame.

*Ayuthia, Thailand*—The best way to see the complex is by river tour in a long-tailed boat (rua hang yao). It is eerie floating among the crumbling ruins. It is easy to get to Ayuthia from Bangkok by boat, bus, or train. Going by boat is the most interesting, but save it for the return to Bangkok when you are going downriver. Going upriver from Bangkok to Ayuthia takes too long. The Oriental Hotel in Bangkok offers a tour to Ayuthia going by bus and returning by boat.

*Lopburi, Thailand*—See Constantine Phaulkon's house near the river. Originally built for the French ambassador, the house was enlarged when Phaulkon moved in. The remaining buildings have a very European apearance. This town was originally the capital of a Mon kingdom in the seventh and eighth centuries. It was later conquered by the Khmers during the glory days of Angkor. A unique fusion of Khmer and Mon art styles can be seen in buildings such as the Wat Prang Sam Yod here. It is a four-hour bus ride from Bangkok's Northern Bus Terminal.

# The Indianization of Southeast Asia

The civilizing influence of Indian Hinduism created most of the great kingdoms of Southeast Asia. India exerted great cultural influence over the states of Southeast Asia, beginning in the second century A.D. The peoples of the region adopted Indian religions (Hinduism, then Buddhism), political structures, art, and customs. The Indian invasion was bloodless, peaceful, and had the support of the people in Southeast Asia.

The attack was led by seagoing Indian traders. Brahmans (Hindu priests) soon followed. The local peoples were impressed with the Indians—they had great gods, wealth, and organization. Local leaders tried Hinduism on for size, liked it, and recommended it for all their people.

One reason leaders and kings took a liking to the Hindu program was the Indian concept of the king as a living god. The kings had been mulling over ways to convince their people of such a concept when the Indians came along and recommended the scheme. The new Hinduized kings were not only responsible for government but also vested with the right and responsibility to protect religion.

As you will recall, Buddhism had arisen in response to Hinduism in India around 500-250 B.C. and was actively promoted by King Asoka. When Buddhism fell into disfavor in India, its supporters looked elsewhere for growth, and many Buddhists came to Southeast Asia in search of converts. Buddhist teachings caught on, and the two transplanted Indian religions lived together harmoniously.

Pick up a modern newspaper in Thailand or Burma. If you have a newspaper from India or Sri Lanka to compare it with, you can see the similarities in the script. Several Southeast Asian peoples adapted their writing from the Indian script, which is generally circular (some call it "bubble writing") because the big leaves they originally used for writing purposes would rip if writers used straight lines and sharp points.

We would know very little about historical Southeast Asia if not for Chinese pilgrims and traders. The Southeast Asians either did not write much down, or the records were lost in the many sackings of rival capitals during the period. Buddhism caught on in China in the sixth century, and some Chinese monks went to India to study the religion fur-

ther. One monk, I-tsing, stopped off in southern Sumatra on his way
to India and studied Sanskrit in the great Buddhist kingdom of Sriwijaya before going on to India to test his Sanskrit.

## Sriwijaya—Phoenicians of the East

When I-tsing left T'ang dynasty China, there were two centers of power
and advanced civilization in Southeast Asia. Sriwijaya was one of the
two. It is easy to see why if we look at the map of the region. There are
only two passages through which the flourishing trade between China
and the Indonesian archipelago and the Indian Ocean could pass, and
southern Sumatra is astride both of them.

The Sriwijaya capital of Palembang became one of the major ports
in the world—and trade meant income and power. If you go to Palembang today, you will probably notice that the city is a good 200 kilometers upriver from the sea. It was no problem for the ships of the time
to get up the river but centuries later, with the advent of the big ships,
Singapore took advantage of its better position and deeper harbor.

Very few concrete artifacts are left of the Sriwijaya Empire. It was a
sea-oriented civilization that did not build great monuments. The
legacy of Sriwijaya can be seen in the dances and dance costumes of the
area. The wedding costumes also reflect Sriwijayan royal court style.

## Majapahit Empire

The Sriwijaya Empire had been centered in Palembang on the huge
Indonesian island of Sumatra. If you are familiar with the Indonesia of
today, however, you are aware that the smaller island of Java is the center of Indonesian civilization. Eighty million Indonesians are crowded
onto Java, and virtually every teenage Indonesian will tell you he or she
wants to go to Java for schooling and work. There is a historical rivalry
between Sumatra and Java, and although Sumatra was the first to
develop, Java was there to pick up the pieces when Sriwijaya was finally
dismembered by Sumatran rivals.

The Majapahit Empire arose on Java in the fourteenth century, and
although it lasted for just over 100 years, it was the first to unify most

of what is today Indonesia (and the Malay Peninsula to the north) and to create an Indonesian identity. The artisans of Majapahit also created a new national style by moving away from Hindu prototypes and reinvigorating the old indigenous folk crafts. The carved reliefs of this period took on a one-dimensional look very reminiscent of the "wayang" shadow puppet plays that remain popular in Indonesia.

Majapahit was a Hindu state, although Hindu and Buddhist symbols were often used to decorate the same structure. Today you can see its Hindu legacy on the island of Bali, one of the few places where subsequent Islamization failed to cover the old Hindu fabric.

## Sites—Majapahit Empire

*Trowulan, Java*—This small village in eastern Java is all that remains at the site of the once mighty Majapahit Empire's capital. The ruins of the brick walls that surrounded the capital and the remains of a few temples are scattered over about eight square miles of countryside. The Trowulan Museum has an extensive and well-displayed collection of Majapahit statues, pottery, and toys. Half a mile south of the museum is an exact reproduction of a Majapahit building.

## The Khmer and Angkor

In the nineteenth century, a French naturalist was led to a site just north of the Tonle Sap River, where Cambodians had said he would find a "lost city." The news of what he found traveled quickly among archaeologists around the world. The ruins of a great city and temple complex were losing ground to the encroaching jungle—massive buildings being torn apart by the roots of huge banyan trees.

The great stone temples and walls the naturalist found were the remains of Angkor, the great capital of the old Khmer kingdom of Kambuja (from which the name Cambodia was derived). Contemporaneous with T'ang (China) times, Kambuja was pieced together out of the fragments of the old Khmer states of Funan and Chenla in 802.

The Khmer people of Kambuja were basically the same people the world now knows as Cambodians or Kampucheans. They had adopted

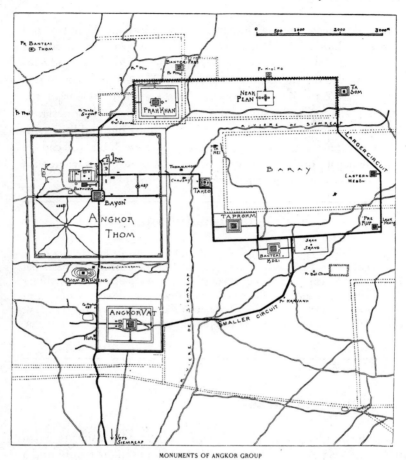

MONUMENTS OF ANGKOR GROUP

Brahmanism (Hinduism) and then Mahayana Buddhism from Indians during the early centuries A.D. and accepted the Hindu idea of the king as a god-king, literally Shiva on earth.

The Khmer god-kings took their position seriously and erected great temple complexes in tribute to their godly selves. The fertility of the middle Mekong Valley meant many taxpayers could be supported and squeezed for money to build huge monuments. The greatest of these was Angkor Wat (in Khmer, "angkor" means "town" and "wat" means "pagoda"). Begun around A.D. 889, Angkor became one of the greatest cities in the world before it was destroyed by the Thai in 1431.

ANGKOR VAT
Longitudinal section, after Fournereau

The Khmers were accomplished artists and architects, and Angkor became one of the most majestic architectural wonders of the world. Unfortunately, this monument is off limits to most of us, because it is located in troubled Kampuchea (the new name for Cambodia). Recently, a few tour operators have been allowed to offer expensive tours to a reopened Angkor.

The great Khmer Kingdom lasted from about A.D. 700 to 1450, when it suffered encroachment by the Thais to the west; the Khmers had become vulnerable because they spent too much on great buildings and works of art. The Khmer capital was moved downriver to Phnom Penh, where it remains today.

If you do not have the good fortune to travel to Angkor but can get to Thailand, some worthwhile remains of the Khmer Kingdom can be seen there. In Lopburi, Thailand, there are several relics of the great Khmer Kingdom. This old town was a Khmer provincial capital during the eleventh and twelfth centuries and is an excellent place to see the beginnings of the synthesis of Khmer and Thai architectural styles.

The Golden Era of Khmer civilization lasted more than 700 years, in part because the kingdom of Champa insulated it from the aggressive Annamite (Vietnamese) Kingdom to the east. The Chams (people of Champa) took the brunt of Annamite expansionism and gave Kambuja time to develop. Today, half a millennium later, the descendants of the Annamites occupy the land of the Khmer (Kampuchea). It is perhaps ironic that many of Kampuchea's Asian neighbors now want to turn Kampuchea into a neutral buffer state between communist Vietnam and democratic Thailand.

## Sites—Khmer Civilization

*Lopburi, Thailand*—The Khmers controlled this area during the tenth to thirteenth centuries and built the Hindu shrines of Wat Prang Sam Yod (since turned into a Buddhist temple) and the Prang Khaek. The three "prangs" or towers of both shrines originally represented the three main Hindu gods of Brahma, Shiva, and Vishnu. Most of the original ornamentation of these buildings has been carted off by thieves.

*Phimai, Thailand*—The Phimai temple here was built by a twelfth-century Khmer king. The Mahayana Buddhist carvings are of exceptional quality. The temples and an open-air museum are open daily from 8:30 a.m. to 4:30 p.m.

## Champa—A Nation that Did Not Survive

The Cham people are still around, but their long-lived kingdom is not. It was swallowed up by the Vietnamese between the tenth and seventeenth centuries. Champa had arisen along the coast of what is now southern Vietnam in the second or third century A.D. Midway between India and China, Champa became the home of great seafaring merchants and prospered from trade.

The Chams, like the Khmers, welcomed the Indian missionaries who brought Brahmanism (Hinduism) and Buddhism. Cham kings took Indian Sanskrit names and gave Sanskrit names such as Indrapura (now Trakieu) and Vijaya (now Binhdinh) to their capitals. Great monuments to the Hindu god Shiva were erected from the seventh to the ninth centuries, but the remains in Vietnam are off-limits to most travelers. The Museum of Tourane, France has one of the best collections of Cham art.

The Chams were continually at war with the Annamites to the north and Khmers to the west. They sacked the Khmer capital of Angkor in the twelfth century but were quickly chased back into Champa by the Khmers, who established a puppet ruler at the Cham capital. The Khmer control was short-lived, however, and it was the expanding Annamites who swallowed Champa. Very little remains of Champa today except the half million Cham-speaking people in the highlands of southern Vietnam and Kampuchea.

## The Burmans

Present-day Burma was virtually without Burmans in A.D. 500. The area was occupied by the Mon people in the south and Pyu people in the north. The people known as Burmans (as opposed to the "Burmese," citizens of modern Burma) were still in eastern Tibet. The Pyus, very closely related to the Burmans, had their capital at Prome in the upper Irrawaddy Delta. The Mons, closely related to the Khmer (Cambodians), had great cities at Thaton and Pegu.

About A.D. 600, the Burmans began drifting south and absorbing the Pyus. By A.D. 800, Prome had been overthrown and the Burman capital established 150 miles to the north at Pagan (pronounced "pah-*gun*" with the stress on the second syllable).

The Mons had earlier adopted Buddhism and a written script from the Indians. When the Burmans, continuing to press southward to the sea, came into contact with the highly cultured Mons, some of Mon civilization rubbed off on them. The Burman King Anauratha was converted to Buddhism, and Mon literature and art were adopted by his court. When King Anauratha's request for copies of the Buddhist canons was turned down by the Mons, the newly converted king had Thaton captured (A.D. 1057) and the canons brought back to Pagan along with the Mon king and his court.

The Mons were not the only ones making diplomatic errors in these parts. Pagan flourished until 1287, when a rebuff of Kublai Khan's representatives resulted in a "visit" by thousands of the Khan's horsemen. One of the world's greatest cities of the time was crushed—and the kingdom with it. But two centuries of glory had unified the territory that comprises modern Burma and merged Burman and Mon culture.

## Burmese Art and Architecture—New Versions of the Indian Stupa

The Burmans were not great painters or sculptors, but what they lacked in ornamentation they made up for in sheer number and size of religious monuments. From India, the Burmans adopted the Indian stupa along with the Theravada Buddhist faith. Stupas soon appeared in such numbers in Burma that within a six-mile radius of the old capital of Pagan, there are remains of over 5,000 religious monuments—most of them stupas.

Indian Buddhist art had already matured into a fixed iconography by the time it accompanied the faith to Burma around the fifth century A.D.—but that did not stop the Burmans and Mons from tinkering with it. Stupas were transformed from the squat, hemispherical, burial mound type preferred by Indians to a soaring, belllike pinnacle version that brings to mind the mythical Mount Meru—the center of the universe. Even the immortals portrayed in Burmese dance wear stupa-like pointed hats.

In Burma, art is synonomous with Buddhist art. The purpose of most art here was—and is—religious. It is rare to find a bas-relief, mural, or sculpture that does not portray a scene from the *Jatakas*, or stories of the Buddha's life. Nonreligious buildings, even the royal palaces, were built of transitory wood (and thus rotted away in the humid climate)—only the stupas and temples were built of stone.

Burmese with means like to sponsor the making of images of the Buddha, since such actions gain the sponsor merit and are believed to facilitate attainment of enlightenment. The typically gold or white images created are relentlessly monotonous and bland. This generic genre is not attributable to a lack of skill among Burmese artisans; rather, the images must not display personality—to do so would diminish their magical power.

Buddhist art and architecture still thrive in Burma as they do in Thailand. New stupas are being built and old ones are continually renewed with fresh gold gilding (an act of merit for donors). A parallel line of secular art and architecture has survived in Burma since the country's military rulers shut the door on the outside world in the 1960s, but one can only hope that the boxy version of socialist architecture will either go away or become fused with the graceful elements of classical Burmese Buddhist architecture.

# Sites—Burma

*Pagan*—The Burmese currently allow tourists into their country for only seven days at a time. I suggest heading directly for the haunting ruins of Pagan, the tenth-century capital of Burma. About 5,000 of the original 50,000 pagodas still stand. Architecturally, the most important pagoda is Anada, which was built in 1091. Its Indian derivation is most evident. Like most temples of the time, the Anada's high ceiling, colossal images, and scarce light are designed to induce a feeling of humility. The archaeological museum here should not be missed. Even to see a fraction of the thirty square kilometers of ruins will require three days.

*Pegu*—The capital of the Mons from the sixth to the eighteenth century. A Burman king completely destroyed the city in 1757, but the 180-foot-long brick and plaster reclining Buddha at the Shwethayaung Temple did, for the most part, survive and is a unique work of Mon art worth seeing.

# The Coming of Islam and the Portuguese

The Java-based Majapahit Empire was pushed off of the Malay Peninsula by the rising power of Islamic Malacca. The king of Malacca had converted to Islam (from Hinduism) around 1419, while the state was under the protection of the Chinese. Malaccan influence enveloped the entire peninsula, and because of this one conversion, the Malay Peninsula is Islamic today.

The Islamic tide was turned back in Europe when the Moors were driven from Spain, but in Asia there is not a major case of any state giving up Islam, once converted. In modern Malaysia it is illegal for other religions to try to convert Muslims.

Ironically, the Muslim success in Malacca was at least partially responsible for bringing the first European colonists to Southeast Asia. The Christian Portuguese had taken Goa on the Indian subcontinent, but they had their eyes on something farther east—the spices of Indonesia. To control the spice trade, the Portuguese needed to control the Straits of Malacca between Sumatra and the Malay Peninsula. Malacca was not only a perfect location from which to control the Straits, but it was a stronghold of Islam. The containment of Islam was at least of secondary importance to the Portuguese. In 1511, the Portuguese took Malacca.

India also served as the jumping-off point for Islam's penetration of Southeast Asia. As we will see, Islam had been brought to India by Turkish and Mughal invaders. Muslim Persian and Indian traders then carried Islam with them as they wandered through Southeast Asia.

By the time the Portuguese arrived in Asia, Islam had converts as far east as the southern Philippines. The Christian Portuguese and the Jesuits failed to dislodge Islam from those areas already claimed by the faith, but they were able to stop further expansion. Today, there are more Muslims in Indonesia than in most nations of the Middle East.

The Muslims were know as "Moors" to the Iberians (Spanish and Portuguese), whose unsuccessful effort to dislodge them from Asia took on the air of a holy war. Although the Islamic faith could not be removed, the Portuguese were successful in replacing the Muslims as the merchants of maritime Asia.

# Sites—Malacca

*Malacca (Melaka), Malaysia*—Although Islam remains the faith of the Malaccan Malays, little else of a tangible nature remains of pre-Portuguese Malacca. The small Malacca Museum exhibits a few weapons of the age. The Sultan's Well near the Bukit China area of the town is said to date from the 1300s.

In the thirteenth century, invaders again came over the mountain passes of northwest India. This time, the invaders were from the Islamic lands of the Middle East. Islamic kingdoms became a feature of India with the founding of the Slave dynasty in north India in 1206. Created by Qutb-ud-din Aibak, a former Turkish slave, the Delhi-centered kingdom was the first of five Turkish dynasties known as the "Delhi Sultanate" which were to rule most of India for 320 years. Aibak, a prolific and inspired builder, constructed India's first mosque, the Quwwat-ul-Islam Masjid (Might of Islam Mosque), and the five-storied Kutb Minar tower in Delhi. You can hear the legacy of Turkish rule in today's Pakistan. The Urdu language spoken there is a mix of Turkish, Persian, and Hindu words.

The Muslim sultans excelled at revenue collection. Nobles were assigned regions of control and given soldiers to collect the taxes, which were fixed at half of income. To avoid letting the nobles establish local power bases from which to challenge the sultan, he rotated his nobles from region to region every few years. Unlike feudal Europe and Japan, the nobles and soldiers were not given title to the land, only the right to collect taxes to pay their salaries.

Think of India not as a country in Asia but as the mini-continent it really is. The Indian subcontinent is not only about the same size as Europe; until relatively recently, it was divided politically, linguistically, and culturally like Europe. As we will see, a British company succeeded in bringing most of the subcontinent together under a single political authority—something the Europeans have been unable to do at home.

# Sites—Muslim India

*Jaunpur in Uttar Pradesh, India*—This city served as the capital of Malik Sarwar, a noble who broke from the Sultanate in the fourteenth century and established his own kingdom for awhile. A unique blend of Indian and Islamic architecture can be seen in many of the high facades of this city today.

*Kutb (Qutb) Minar in Delhi*—The first of its kind in India. Also erected by Aibak around A.D. 1200, this red sandstone tower of Islamic victory is over seventy-two meters high, and it used to be higher. To avoid the tourist buses, arrive just after the tower opens at sunrise or just before it closes at sunset.

*Quwwat-ul-Islam Masjid in Delhi*—In keeping with Islamic tradition, the carvings are primarily geometric patterns. Built by Aibak in 1193 (before he proclaimed himself Sultan), the mosque is made of pieces of twenty-seven Hindu temples he had demolished. An iron pillar with fourth-century Sanskrit inscriptions stands in a courtyard here; it is a mystery where the pillar came from or how it was made.

# Meanwhile... Events Outside of Asia

## Sui and T'ang dynasty in China, Silla in Korea: A.D. 500-1000

—Dark Ages grip Europe (500-1000)
—Vikings invade Ireland (620)
—Muhammad, founder of Islam, dies (632)
—Muslims take Egypt (639)
—Moors (Muslims) invade Spain (711)
—Papal States are founded in Italy (756)
—Charlemagne is King of the Franks (771-814)
—Acropolis of Zimbabwe built (ca. 850)
—Mayans move into Mexico's Yucatán Peninsula (ca. 900)
—Nigerian kingdom of Hausa founded (900)
—Polynesian Maoris discover New Zealand (ca. 950)
—The Viking, Eric the Red, settles in Greenland (981)

## Northern Sung to Ming times: 1000-1500

—High Middle Ages in Europe (1000-1500)
—The Viking, Leif Ericsson, explores coast of North America (1002)
—Danes rule England (1016-1042)
—Ghana Empire dominates West Africa (920-1240)
—Battle of Hastings (1066)
—The Crusades (1100-1250)
—Demise of the Toltec Empire in Mexico (1150)
—Magna Carta (1215)
—The plague kills one out of every four Europeans (1300-1400)
—Inca Empire in Peru (1440)
—Hundred Years' War between England and France (1338-1453)
—Christopher Columbus crosses Atlantic and stumbles onto the
  West Indies and South America (1492-1498)

# 7

# The Colonial Age (A.D. 1500-1850)

Vasco da Gama's three small vessels glided into view of the Malabar Coast of India in 1498. Eleven months had passed since they set sail from Lisbon's harbor and headed south for the Cape of Good Hope at Africa's southern extreme. A long voyage across the vast Indian Ocean had brought them within sight of their objective—the spice market of south India. Da Gama dropped anchor near a small village just north of Calicut, a center of pepper production.

The round-trip took da Gama more than two years, but when he unloaded his cargo of spice in Lisbon, it brought 60 times the cost of the voyage. Fifteenth-century Europe was crazy for spice—the only thing, in the absence of refrigerators, that could make rancid meat palatable.

Europeans knew that spices came from south India and the "Spice Islands" of what is today Indonesia, but they had been forced to rely upon the far-ranging Arab merchants who controlled the trade routes. The enterprising merchants of Venice bought the spices from the Arabs at Middle East ports. By the time the precious spices reached the Western Europeans, they commanded a high price.

The Western European aristocracy, which could afford meat, was sick of the unpleasantness of old meat and sick of paying inflated prices to the Venetian merchants, who had a stranglehold on the spice trade. There had to be a way, the Europeans thought, to cut the greedy merchants and the "heathen" Muslim traders out of the business. Enter the Portuguese—and then the Spanish, Dutch, French, and English.

Europeans began trickling into Asia in ever-increasing numbers after da Gama and his fellow Portuguese set up a trading post on the Indian coast. India and China had seen a few European traders before (such as the Polo family of the twelfth century), and had suffered and absorbed invaders such as the Aryans, Mongols, Turks, and others. But unlike previous invaders, who always seemed to come out of northern mountains, the Renaissance Europeans came from the south, by sea— ship by ship.

The great Portuguese navigators did not think of themselves as invaders but as explorers in the name of the Portuguese crown. Although a few priests came along to conquer what souls could be found, it was business that the Europeans were after. There were a few glitches at first—the subtropical Indians were not sure they wanted the woolens and timepieces the Europeans brought to trade, but the Indians had no trouble moving their silk and cotton fabrics, tobacco, and spice—all highly prized by the Europeans.

## Renaissance Brings Europeans to Asia

At the same time that the Portuguese were making their first tentative forays along the coasts of western Africa around the turn of the fifteenth century, Chinese ships were visiting the east coast of Africa. Large armadas of as many as sixty-two ships were sent forth by the Ming court to impress the people of the southern seas with China's might.

Why didn't the Chinese fleets sail on around the Cape of Good Hope to Europe? Why did mighty China, with a population of 120 million, wait for Portugal and Spain (with a combined population of only 8 million) to land on her doorstep? It is no coincidence that Europeans began coming to Asia at the very time that the cultural rebirth known as the Renaissance was flowering at home.

At the turn of the fifteenth century, Europe entered an explosive age of political, spiritual, and economic revolution, later dubbed the "Renaissance" or "rebirth." Europeans began to think of themselves as masters of their own destiny rather than as pawns of fate. The power of the Church receded and secular individualism, the pursuit of wealth, and science became the rage. The new ways of thinking and technological know-how could not be contained—the Europeans were driven out of Europe by the force of their own revolution.

The Europeans of the fifteenth century had the technical competence, the weapons (new cannons and ships), and the determination to go where they saw opportunity. At the time, Asia was the Land of Opportunity. Ironically, the Europeans used the Asian inventions of the compass, gunpowder, and astrolabe (primitive sextant) to force their way into Asia. As a vigorous Europe exploded out of the Dark Ages, Asia was entering a vulnerable period of withdrawal and fragmentation. The Ming rulers, under attack by northern nomads, ordered a dramatic reversal of their expansive foreign relations. Chinese sailors were told to stick close to Chinese land and the Chinese were forbidden to leave their own country. In Southeast Asia, Khmers, Burmans, Thais, and Mons fought one another. India was fragmented as rival Muslim and Hindu states fought for territory.

## The Portuguese—Thin Edge of the European Wedge

Two years after Vasco da Gama landed near Calicut, India, Pedro Cabral (another Portuguese adventurer) tried a new route to India by going around South America. In the process he stumbled onto what would become Brazil. The language of Brazil today is Portuguese, thanks to the spice-seeking merchants of sixteenth-century Portugal.

The Portuguese were after souls as well as spice. With the grand concept dancing in their heads of a world empire ruled by Christ, the Portuguese dispatched missionaries alongside their traders. The most famous missionary-adventurer was St. Francis Xavier, one of the founders of the Catholic Jesuit Order. Francis was sent forth to save the Orient in 1542. Most of Francis' efforts were concentrated along the Malabar and Coromandel coasts of India, but he also sought converts in Japan and Indonesia—but with little luck. He was on his way to China when he died off the coast of the Middle Kingdom and was buried on a small island nearby. His body was later reburied in Malacca (Malaysia) and then re-reburied in Goa (India) by his countrymen, who wanted his remains closer to Portuguese strongholds. The Catholic Portuguese were particularly determined to turn back the tide of Islam in Asia. For five centuries (1000-1500) the Portuguese and the Spaniards had fought to eject the Arab emirs (Moors) from the Iberian Peninsula. The last Islamic emirate in Spain was not defeated until 1492, just six years before da Gama's arrival in India.

The port of Goa was seized by the Portuguese in 1510 (India was too divided to resist) and became their Asian operations headquarters. During the sixteenth century, the Portuguese buildings in the city of Old Goa rivaled the splendors of Lisbon. This area of 9 million people on India's west coast remained a Portuguese colony until the Indians forcibly removed the Portuguese in 1961.

The Portuguese moved quickly to control the Straits of Malacca by capturing the port of Malacca (Malaysia) a year after taking Goa. They also established a trade center at Macao, a small peninsula on the coast of south China, in 1557. By the nineteenth century, Portugal's Asian empire was in a state of decay, as was its relative position among the European powers. The first to get into Asia, Portugal will be the last to leave. In 1999, two years after Hong Kong is scheduled to revert to China, Portugal will hand Macao back to China.

The rise and fall of European dominance in Asia spanned 450 years. It began with Vasco de Gama's landing on the coast of India in 1498, but it was not until the mid-nineteenth-century that colonial empire-building became the European objective. European power reached its height in the nineteenth century, when the British became the dominant power in Asia.

**The Portuguese in Asia—Important Dates**

1498—Vasco da Gama reaches Calicut, India
1511—Portuguese take Malacca
1549—Francis Xavier introduces Catholicism to Japan
1557—Portuguese establish a trade center at Macao
1849—Portuguese claim jurisdiction over Macao

# Sites—The Portuguese at Cochin, India

Vasco da Gama returned to India for a second time in 1502 and founded a trading post at Cochin. In modern Cochin you will find the following remnants of medieval Portugal, mostly in the Fort Cochin area.

*St. Francis Church*—Vasco da Gama is buried here on the grounds of the oldest European church in India. The church later passed through the hands of the Dutch and British as they, in turn, occupied Cochin.

*Dutch Palace*—Built by the Portuguese in 1557 as a gift for the locl Raja. The two-storied building surrounds a courtyard housing a Hindu temple. The building sports some of the best Hindu murals in India. A good place to see how the Rajas lived. It is called the "Dutch" Palace because the Dutch renovated it in the seventeenth century. Bring "fast" film of 400 ASA+ because flash photography is prohibited inside.

*Jewish synagogue*—Just across the street from the Dutch Palace is the oldest Jewish synagogue in India. Built in 1567, it was badly damaged by the Portuguese in 1662. The Jewish community on the Malabar Coast dates from about A.D. 50.

# Sites—Portuguese Goa

*Se Cathedral*—Built for the Portuguese Dominicans over a period of sixty years, starting in 1562. A fine example of Portuguese Gothic architecture.

*Basilica of Bom Jesus*—This is where the body of St. Francis Xavier lays in rest. His body is exposed to view once every ten years on the anniversary of his death. For this event make plans for December 1994 and 2004. If you cannot make it to Goa, you can see his right hand in the Church of Gesu in Rome where it was taken by the Catholic Church so the Saint might be nearer the seat of Catholicism.

---

## The Dutch—European Entrepreneurs in Asia

The Dutch came hard on the heels of the Portuguese, setting up commercial trade ventures on the Indian and Ceylonese coasts. By the mid-eighteenth century, they had concentrated their power in Ceylon and the East Indies (Indonesia). The British forced them out of Ceylon during the European Napoleonic wars.

Unlike the Portuguese, the Dutch did not come to Asia to proselytize—they came to trade. By the sevententh century, they controlled the spice-rich Indonesian archipelago, and Dutch coffee and sugar plantations covered the island of Java. The Dutch did not leave Indonesia until the Japanese invaded in 1942—but even today, foreigners in Indonesia are often greeted as "Belanda!" (Hollander).

## The Dutch in Asia—Important Dates

1596—Dutch arrive at Banten, Indonesia
1602—Dutch East Indies Company chartered
1624—Dutch establish forts and trade center on Taiwan

---

# Sites—The Dutch in Asia

*Malacca, Malaysia*—The Dutch controlled Malacca for 150 years. Stadthuys, their pink seventeenth-century town hall, still stands in the main square of Malacca. The nearby bright red Christ Church was built by the Dutch in 1753.

*Fort Zeelandia, Tainan, Taiwan*—The Dutch controlled most of Taiwan for thirty-seven years (1624-1661) and set up their headquarters at Tainan in southern Taiwan. The remains of the Dutch Fort Providentia (called "Chihkan Tower" by the Taiwanese) are near the city center, and a reconstruction of their Fort Zeelandia ("Anping") can be seen near the sea to the west of Tainan. So little is left after three centuries of typhoons and earthquakes that I recommend seeing the forts only if you are in the area.

---

## England, Inc.

The English who began to appear in the East were not civil servants, the military, or even the clergy, but rather the English East India Company's traders and clerks. In 1707, England gave a commercial monopoly for trade with India to the East India Company, a monopoly that persisted until 1813.

While the Portuguese strategy was to control the seas with superior maritime skills and hold a few strategic ports, the English and the other Europeans added inland areas to their area of control.

The city of Madras took root around the walls of the English fort of St. George. Bombay was presented to the East India Company by Charles II, who received the city from Portugal as part of his wife's dowry. The third strategic English settlement was Fort William near Calcutta.

Merchants controlled the English settlements in India; governors were elected by councils of merchants, and affairs were administered by company directors in London.

In 1756, the Indians, with a little help from the French, attacked and took Fort William in Calcutta and threw 146 Englishmen and women into a tiny, airless prison cell, where all but twenty-three died overnight. The cell became known to British historians as the "Black Hole of Calcutta."

A former expatriate clerk cum military commander, Robert Clive, regained the upper hand for the British a year later when he defeated the Indians and their French supporters at Plassey, about 170 kilometers north of Calcutta. Within a year Clive was governor of Bengal.

In 1857, the British made the mistake of introducing a rifle cartridge greased with pork or beef fat that had to be bitten before use. Biting into beef or pork is anathema to Hindus and Muslims and when they found out what they had been sinking their teeth into, they mutinied and killed their British officers. It took a year and a half for the British to crush what became known as the Sepoy Mutiny.

The British controlled more of India than any previous ruler, native or foreign. From the beginning of their involvement in India, the British objective was finding customers for British products. India, with its huge population, was a gold mine of potential customers. Eyeing the Indians as customers, the British set out to educate them and create an industrial infrastructure for their country—so that the Indian might be an even better customer with money to spend.

## The English in India—Important Dates

1612—first English trade center in India at Surat
1639—Fort St. George established on land ceded by Madras ruler
1668—Charles II gives Bombay to East India Company
1691—Fort William established near Calcutta
1707—English East India Company formed
1756—"Black Hole of Calcutta" incident
1798—Ceylon made a crown colony
1813—East India Company's monopoly on India trade terminated
1835—English replaces Persian as official language of India
1857—Sepoy Mutiny
1858—sovereignty over India transferred from Company to crown
1877—Queen Victoria proclaimed Empress of India

---

# Sites—England in Asia

*Calcutta, India*—This great city grew up around a fort the English established on the Hooghly River. For more information see "Calcutta" in the "Exploring Modern Asia" section.

---

## The French in Asia

French, rather than English, might be one of the official languages of India today if French support for its colonists had not wavered. The French had opened a trading center at Surat, India in 1668, and six years later they purchased the port of Pondicherry on southeast India's coast. By the mid-eighteenth-century the British had driven the French from India, and the French turned their attention to their Indochina colonies. The French and English struggle for supremacy in Europe during the War of the Austrian Succession (1740-1748) had spilled over into Asia. In an ultimately unsuccessful bid to outflank British expansion in India, the French governor of Pondicherry, Joseph Dupleix, used

Indian troops called "sepoys" to expand French "protection" over the Indian state of Hyderabad. He taxed Indian rulers to pay the French costs of this protection.

### The French in Asia—Important Dates

1664—French East India Company founded
1668—first French trading center opened in India at Surat
1674—French purchase port of Pondicherry, India

---

## Sites—French in Asia

*Pondicherry, India*—The French did not abandon this city on the east coast of India until 1954. Once the capital of their settlements in India, it was divided into a French (white) section and a Black Town for the Indians.

Many old colonial-style structures remain.

---

### Europeans Arrive in China

European arrogance ran headlong into Chinese conceit. The Chinese called their country "Zhongguo" or "Middle Kingdom" and had long thought of themselves as the center of the world. Their recent over-throw of the Mongolian-controlled Yuan dynasty and expulsion of these foreign rulers from Chinese soil added to the nationalistic fervor. To the Chinese, now more than ever, foreigners were uncivilized bump-kins and China demanded tribute from them all.

The Ming-dynasty Chinese did not need lessons in imperialism— they took northern Vietnam and demanded tribute from kingdoms around the Indian Ocean. Only the renewed pressure of nomadic tribes to the north reined in Chinese expansionism.

### The Manchu—Foreigners Take China Again

The Manchus from the northeast seized Peking in 1644 and proclaimed the founding of the Ching (Qing) dynasty. The last Ming emperor com-

AN IMPERIAL AUDIENCE.

mitted suicide. For the second time in China's long history, foreigners took control of all China.

Ming loyalists fled the Chinese mainland for the large island of Taiwan, located about 100 miles off the coast of Fujian Province. There they were led in a futile attempt to retake the mainland by the son of an ex-pirate. By 1683, China had annexed Taiwan.

The Manchus made a few changes; for instance, men were required to adopt the Manchu hair queue as a sign of loyalty to the throne. But many things—most important, the effective Mandarin bureaucracy—did not change.

The Manchu also adopted the eternal Chinese view that all people outside of the Middle Kingdom were inferior. When it became obvious that the Europeans poking around the edges of China were not seeking to pay tribute but had come with the notion to trade on terms of equality, the Manchus sought to turn the Europeans back. Neither were the Manchus impressed with the gifts which King George III had sent to Emperor Chien Lung in 1792. The emperor wrote to the king:

> Swaying the wide world, I have but one aim in view, namely to maintain a perfect governance and to fulfill the duties of the state. Strange and costly objects do not interest me. I have no use for your country's products. It behooves you, O King, to respect my

sentiments and to display even greater devotion and loyalty in the future, so that by perpetual submission to our throne, you may secure peace and prosperity for your country hereafter. Tremblingly obey and show no negligence.

### The Opium Wars

China assumed increased importance to the British after their American colonies were lost to revolutionaries. The Manchu had restricted English trade to the south China city of Canton in southern China. English merchants found that selling opium to Chinese drug addicts was an easy way to finance the purchase of silk, tea, and other Chinese products the folks back in Europe wanted. When the Chinese objected to English efforts to facilitate the opium habit among Chinese, the English attacked and defeated China in the First Opium War (1839-1842). The English were not satisfied with the many concessions they extracted from Peking (including the ceding of Hong Kong to Britain). In 1856, with the help of France, they started the Second Opium War. The two European powers captured Peking and won more trading concessions. In a particularly cruel maneuver, reminiscent of what the British had done to Washington, D.C., in the War of 1812, the Imperial Summer Palace was torched for good measure.

## Vijayanagar—Great Hindu Empire of India

Refugees from the onslaught of Muslim invaders in the north of India established the Hindu city of Vijayanagar (City of Victory) in 1336. On the banks of the Tungabhadra River in south India, the city expanded into the largest Hindu empire in history—controlling most of south India. The capital city was home to half a million people, many of whom were involved in the spice and cotton trades.

The Vijayanagar Empire did for Hinduism what the earlier Mauryan Empire of Asoka had done for Buddhism. Hindu arts and learning were patronized by the Vijayanagar rulers. Despite the religious fervor of the empire's rulers, they were tolerant of other religions and Jainism prospered under their protection. The Vijayanagarians revitalized the waning popularity of the gods Vishnu and Shiva. The huge Dravidian-style halls of the city were roofed with immense stone slabs supported by pillars sporting *shaktis*, dancing girls, monsters, and rearing horses.

A confederacy of south Indian sultans smashed the empire in 1565. Soon after their victory, the sultans themselves were gobbled up by the Moghal Empire of the north.

# Sites—Vijayanagar

You can find what is left of Vijayanagar at present-day Hampi in Karnataka State. Although about equidistant between Goa and Bangalore, Hampi is easiest to reach by bus from Bangalore (via Hospet). The ruins are found among huge, rounded boulders that cover the hillsides. Allow a day and a half for walking around the scattered ruins—and arrange your itinerary to be there at sunset when the ruins and boulders turn red. Do not miss the following sites, either.

*Vittala Temple*—Stone chariot and sculpture.

*Purandara Dasara Mndapa Temple*—Nearby are ruins of a stone bridge that spanned the river.

## Moghal Empire—Muslim Rulers of North India

The Muslim Moghuls (an Indian term for "Mongol"), like the Turks and the Aryans before them, invaded India from the area of present-day Afghanistan. Although Delhi had been pillaged by the Moghul commander Timur (Tamerlane) in 1399, it was not until 1526 that the Moghuls took control of a fragmented north India. For most of 600 years, Muslims controlled most of north India, but their control never reached into the Hindu-dominated southern tip of the peninsula. Although always a minority in predominately Hindu India, the Moghul rulers succeeded in maintaining political power until the British replaced them in the nineteenth century. Babur, the founder of the dynasty, claimed descent from Genghis Khan and Tamerlane, but it was Akbar, the third ruler, who distinguished himself. During his reign (1556-1605) Akbar protected cows, employed Hindus, and married

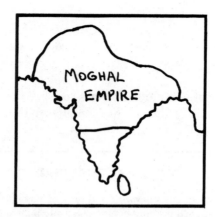

into Rajput families. His political and religious tolerance gained him the respect of his 100 million (mostly Hindu) subjects. Disillusioned with Islam, he disavowed the faith and proclaimed his own religion created from Islamic, Christian, and Persian elements. The greatest Moghal ruler, Akbar brought most of north India under his rule but was surprisingly hostile to Islam. He sought to understand the various religions, including Christianity, but he did not embrace any religion wholeheartedly. He allowed his subjects to practice the rites and customs of their religions freely.

## Sites—Moghal India

*Nizamuddin in Delhi*—This village is the oldest living example of Moghal India. If you are tired of ruins and want to experience "medieval" Muslim India, you can do so in the narrow lanes of this Muslim community, which is chockfull of fine specimens of Indo-Islamic architecture. The village surrounds Nizamuddin Shrine in the southeast part of Delhi City.

*Taj Mahal*—This mausoleum in Agra, India was built by Akbar's son, Jahangir, for his wife. It took 20,000 laborers fifteen years to build.

### The Sikhs

Near the end of the Delhi Sultanate a group in the Punjab area split off from mainstream Hinduism to form a monotheistic, faith-stressing

doctrine. Led by Nanak (1469-1538), the militant Sikhs (pronounced "seeks") dominated the Punjab region within a century of their founding. A succession of ten leaders, or "gurus," consolidated the faith, completed its sacred texts, and established the city of Amritsar as the faith's religious center. Famous for their military prowess, Sikh regiments later played a large role in the British-Indian armies and today even the U.S. armed forces extends special permission to Sikh-American soldiers to wear their turbans, beards, bangles, and hair daggers as part of their uniform.

## Meanwhile . . . Events Outside of Asia

### Age of European Expansion: 1500-1850

—The European Renaissance (1500-1600)
—Leonardo da Vinci (1452-1519)
—Michelangelo (1475-1564)
—Gregorian calendar introduced (1582)
—Spanish Armada defeated by English (1588)
—Turks conquer north coast of Africa (1554-1556)
—Magellan's expedition circumnavigates world (1522)
—Hernando de Soto finds the Mississippi River (1541)
—Colony of Virginia started by English (1607)

—Brazil taken from Dutch by Portuguese (1654)
—Peter I is Czar of Russia (1689-1725)
—Boston Tea Party (1773)
—Americans declare independence from Britain (1776)
—First British convicts exiled to Australia (1788)
—French Revolution (1789)
—Napoleon Bonaparte as emperor (1804-1814)
—Zulu Empire rises in Africa (1818)
—Simon Bolivar wins independence for Colombia (1819)
—Irish potato famine (1840-1850)
—California Gold Rush (1848)

# 8

# Modernizing Asia (A.D. 1850-Today)

The political fragmentation and isolation that had gripped Asia at the turn of the fifteenth century would not go away—a slumbering and victimized Asia coasted through the nineteenth century and into the twentieth. In the first half of the nineteenth century, China's Ch'ing rulers spent the nation's defense monies on luxuries, the Moghul Empire of India was falling apart, and Japan languished in self-imposed isolation. But pockets of modernization began to appear in the later half of the nineteenth century—especially in Japan. European domination of Asia approached and passed its zenith during this period, only to be replaced by the Japanese version of imperialism. Japan first invaded China in the 1930s and then engulfed the Pacific Rim, from Alaska to Indonesia. The colonial period was a comparatively short phase in the long history of Asia, but it drastically reshaped the character of the continent and its people.

## British India—The Honeymoon's Over

The British honeymoon in India ended in 1857. A new rifle cartridge was introduced that required the rifleman to bite into it before use. The

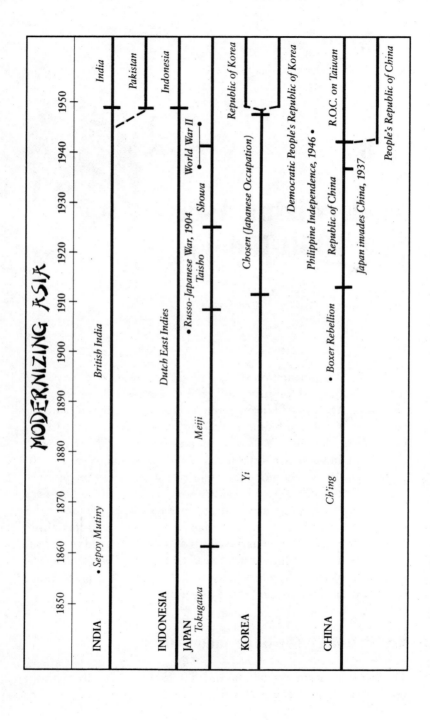

MODERNIZING ASIA

| | 1850 | 1860 | 1870 | 1880 | 1890 | 1900 | 1910 | 1920 | 1930 | 1940 | 1950 |
|---|---|---|---|---|---|---|---|---|---|---|---|

**INDIA** • Sepoy Mutiny — British India — India / Pakistan

**INDONESIA** — Dutch East Indies — Indonesia

**JAPAN** Tokugawa — Meiji — Taisho • Russo-Japanese War, 1904 — Shōwa — World War II

**KOREA** Yi — Chosen (Japanese Occupation) — Republic of Korea / Democratic People's Republic of Korea

Philippine Independence, 1946 •

**CHINA** Ch'ing • Boxer Rebellion — Republic of China — Japan invades China, 1937 — R.O.C. on Taiwan / People's Republic of China

SEPOY REBELS BEING SHOT FROM THE MOUTHS OF THE CANNON

many Hindu and Muslim Sepoys (native Indian soldiers in the British army) in the military service did not necessarily object to biting cartridges, but when they heard that the cartridges were greased with pork or beef fat (anathema to Muslims and Hindus, respectively), they mutinied. The mutiny lasted a year and a half.

Afterward, the British-Indian relationship was never the same. British interest in pushing social change and self-government was replaced by bitterness and distrust. A policy of noninterference in the socioreligious affairs of India was instituted. The British fervor to force change in India was gone. As the mutiny was crushed, the British Crown took control of India away from the East India Company. London now reigned over more of the subcontinent than had any native or alien power.

The British began to relish the idea of great empire in the East. The phrase "White Man's Burden" was bandied about private clubs from London to Calcutta during the later nineteenth century. The apparent ease with which the British controlled their subjects became justification for a conviction that it was the right and responsibility of Europeans to extend their rule and culture to the "lesser peoples" of the world. In 1877 British Prime Minister Disraeli had Queen Victoria proclaimed "Empress of India."

But Indian political opposition to colonial rule grew as Britain tightened its grip on her crown jewel. Indians educated in Western political ideology instigated a struggle for independence. In 1915, Mohandis

Gandhi returned to India from South Africa, where he had practiced law, to lead a nonviolent revolution for independence. Gandhi's weapon was noncooperation with the British rulers of India, backed by a boycott of British goods. Wizened and weary Britain began to prepare for Indian independence.

In the late 1930s, a major problem developed over what to do with the 90 million Muslims (a minority) in India. The Muslims were demanding a partition of India into seperate Hindu and Muslim states, but Gandhi and the Congress Party strenuously opposed partition.

Although Muslim and Hindu enmity cannot be blamed entirely on the Raj (the British colonial government), it is perhaps ironic that British efforts to rid themselves of the "India problem" were complicated by their own nineteenth-century policy of discrimation against Muslims. After the Sepoy Mutiny of 1857, the British tried to preempt Indian unity by favoring Hindus over Muslims for job and education opportunities. They succeeded. World War II further delayed Indian independence, but upon the Allied victory, Britain set up a joint Hindu-Muslim administration in India to prepare for independence. Britain sent Lord Mountbatten to India to settle Hindu-Muslim disagreements over a post-independence government, and in 1947, realizing the intransigence of the Muslim leaders, Mountbatten arranged a hasty partition of India into a majority Hindu India and a largely Muslim Pakistan. The two new nations became independent on 15 August 1947.

# Japan Opens Up

Against its will, Japan was forced to come out and play with the West. In 1863 the American Commodore Matthew Perry sailed up the coast near Tokyo (called "Edo" at the time), delivered a demand for a trade treaty, and sailed off, saying he would be back in the spring for an answer. The shogun reluctantly accepted the ultimatum. Perry would inadvertently become the catalyst for the end of both feudalism and the military government of Japan.

Since A.D. 1192, Japan had been ruled by a succession of hereditary military dictators called "shoguns." Since 1603 the Tokugawa family

In 1904, the Japanese defeated Russian troops stationed in the Far East and captured the Russian-controlled Chinese city of Port Arthur.

had maintained the shogunate and had imposed a strict policy of isolationism on Japan. Japan was effectively quarantined—Japanese were not permitted to travel abroad and foreigners were unwelcome in Japan.

Powerful nobles, opposed to the shogun's opening up of Japan to the West, convinced Emperor Mutsuhito to overthrow the last shogun in 1868. They had hoped the emperor would again bring down the curtain around their islands, but Emperor Mutsuhito did just the opposite. He took the name of "Meiji" (Enlightened Rule) and embarked on an incredible reorientation program for Japan. Westernization and industrialization were "in." By the time of his death in 1912, Emperor Meiji had changed Japan into one of the most powerful nations in the world.

Tokyo is still in its infancy as a capital city. Shogun Tokugawa Ieyasu selected Tokyo (Edo) as his capital in 1601. The powerless emperors stayed on in the official capital of Kyoto (which means "capital"). When power was restored to the Imperial family in 1868, there was indecision about moving the capital. The decision was fraught with symbolic implications—would the new emperor signal rejection of foreign overtures by moving the capital to an inland city such as Osaka, or rather to Edo near the trading port of Yokahama? In a fit of decisive ambiguity, the emperor "established" (not "moved") a capital at Edo and renamed it Tokyo, (Eastern Capital). During Emperor Meiji's life, Kyoto continued to be a ceremonial capital. When he died, he chose to be buried at Kyoto.

In 1904, Japan and Russia went to war over trade rights and influence in Korea and Manchuria (part of China). The Japanese defeated the relatively few Russian troops stationed in the Far East and captured the Russian-controlled Chinese city of Port Arthur. The Russian Baltic fleet sailed around Africa and Asia to meet, and be annihilated by, the Japanese navy in the Korean Strait. In 1905 U.S. President Theodore Roosevelt brought the two sides together at Portsmouth, New Hampshire where a peace was hammered out. Part of Japan's prize was the southern half of Russia's Sakhalin Island. Forty years later, Japan lost Sakhalin, and a few other former Japanese islands to the Soviet Union as a result of World War II.

TOKIO—TYPES AND COSTUMES.

## Sites—Meiji Tokyo

*Ueno Park in Tokyo*—The authority of the shogunate had already been surrendered when the forces supporting the emperor arrived in Edo on a rainy day in May, 1868. In the tradition of the "fighting spirit" so beloved by Japanese, the shogun's loyalists refused to accept capitulation willingly and made a final, futile stand on the heights of present-day Ueno Park. The loyalist's defenses were breached at Kuro-mon (Black Gate), near the present main entrance to the park. Kaneji Temple, just southwest of the Uguisudani train station, is where the shoguns of the Tokugawa era came to worship and relax. The original temple was destroyed in the battle of 1868—the high-roofed temple that stands in Ueno today was moved there from Gumma Prefecture. Six shoguns rest within a stone wall in the cemetery surrounding Kaneji Temple, their graves marked by a bronze monument. Ueno Park now houses the three buildings of the Tokyo National Museum (the Horyuji Homotsukan Building contains the most treasured ancient artifacts) and the National Museum of Western Art, complete with Rodin bronzes.

*Meiji Mura, Nagoya*—The best collection of Meiji Age memorabilia is at Meiji Mura open-air museum near Nagoya (central Japan). Reconstructed buildings show Western influence on the lifestyle of the time. The lobby of the Frank Lloyd Wright-designed Imperial Hotel was moved here from Tokyo. Some of Japan's first trains and trolleys are preserved here.

*Meiji Shrine, Tokyo*—A forested garden-park and shrine built to deify Emperor Meiji as a Shinto god. The buildings are of the classical Shinto style of magnificent simplicity. Emperor Meiji's six-horse carriage is on display in the Memorial Picture Gallery in the center of the park. The iris garden on the shrine grounds was designed by Emperor Meiji for his empress.

## China—Rebellions and Revolution

Fed up with foreign interference in China, and led by a group called "The Society of Harmonious Fists" (known to Westerners as "Boxers"), many Chinese revolted in the late 1890s, killing thousands of Chinese Christians and more than 200 Westerners. In Peking, the Boxers attacked and surrounded the foreign legations for fifty-five days, until an international expedition of soldiers from Britain, France, Germany,

Italy, Austria, Russia, Japan, and the United States fought its way to the rescue. As punishment, the foreign powers levied huge fines (compensations) on China.

### End of the Empire

The Manchus had ruled China since 1644 in the guise of the Ch'ing dynasty, and by the end of the nineteenth century their rule was weakened by internal corruption and foreign domination. Chinese dissatisfaction with imperial ways and the foreign exploitation of their country exploded into a rebellion in October 1911. Within three months a Republic of China government was proclaimed and Dr. Sun Yat-sen elected its president.

## Sites—Ch'ing Dynasty China

*Shenyang, China*—Formerly known by its Manchurian name, "Mukden," this city was both the birthplace of the Manchu nation in the seventeenth century and a focus of the Russo-Japanese War of 1905. The Manchu Imperial Palace at Shenyang was completed in 1636 and provides a glimpse into Manchu court life in the years before they conquered China and established the Ch'ing dynasty. The walled, fifteen-acre palace was recently restored and turned into a museum of Ch'ing dynasty artifacts and art. This is a complete imperial palace complex, featuring over seventy buildings with brilliant yellow glazed tile roofs.

## Communism Comes to Asia

Within two years of the 1917 Russian Revolution, Russian Marxist missionaries arrived in China. Their doctrine of Marxism was the same but the pitch was changed to appeal to a different audience. The Chinese, sick of unequal treaties forced upon them by Western powers, were receptive when early Chinese Communists like Mao Zedong talked of throwing out the imperialists.

Rivalry between the Chinese Communist Party and the Kuomintang

Party (Nationalists) of Sun Yat-sen and Chaing Kai-shek prolonged China's turmoil for decades. The two parties united against the invading Japanese from 1937 to 1945 but quickly resumed hostilities after the Japanese defeat. Within four years the strife-torn Kuomintang was forced to retreat (along with over 2 million mainlanders) to the offshore island of Taiwan. Thirty years after communism was introduced to China, its proponents claimed victory.

China was a latecomer to the communist club. Mongolia became the world's second communist state in 1924, when the Soviets helped the Mongolian People's Revolutionary Party establish the Mongolian People's Republic.

## Sites—Communism in Asia

*Yan'an, China*—After two and a half years of wandering through China on the "Long March" to find refuge from the pursuing Kuomintang forces, the communists' Eighth Route Army reached the small town of Yan'an. Mao Zedong (Mao Tse-tung), Zhou Enlai, and Zhu De lived in the cliffside caves here with their compatriots. It was here that they changed their failed, urban-based revolution into a successful, peasant-oriented movement. The caves Mao lived in from 1937 to 1947 are preserved as museums, exhibiting Mao's belongings and artifacts of the Long March period.

## New Nations Arise

Imperial Japan wiped East and Southeast Asia clean of Western colonialists during World War II, as the Land of the Rising Sun sought to create its own empire. When the Western powers finally corralled Japan's militarists and sent them packing back home, the former colonies did not put out the welcome mat for the old colonialists. The Asians were in no mood for any kind of imperialism, Asian or Western.

Upon Japan's surrender, the Dutch tried to retake their former colony (the Netherlands East Indies), but the Indonesians resisted, won over world opinion, and achieved independence in 1948. America moved quickly to grant independence to the Philippines on July 4, 1946. Burma's independence was negotiated peacefully with Britain and realized in 1948. The French returned to Vietnam and fought the Viet Minh nationalists for seven years, until the former colonists were forced to admit military defeat in 1954. New nation-states were popping up all over Asia.

## Birth of Malaysia

Malaysia is a relatively new Asian nation contructed out of loose political parts of the old British Empire in the East. British colonialists had found the Malay Peninsula very much unassembled in the nineteenth century: Muslim sultans controlled small states throughout the Malay Peninsula and north Borneo. Adept political maneuverings by the British changed the sultanates first into protectorates, then into colonies.

The British were driven out of their colonies on the Malay Peninsula, Singapore, and north Borneo by the Japanese during World War II. As soon as the Japanese laid down their guns in 1945, the British returned, but in a weakened position. The British were ready to grant Malaya independence, and for eleven years the British turned the reins of government over, step-by-step, to Malaya while simultaneously supressing an indigenous communist insurgency.

The states on the Malay Peninsula were molded together to form independent Malaya (Federation of Malaya) in 1957. Six years later, the British colonies of Singapore, North Borneo (Sabah), and Sarawak were added to Malaya to form the new nation of Malaysia. Singapore dropped out of the union in 1965. It was a divorce based upon incompatibility—Singapore was too Chinese (76%, to be exact).

Malays were at a disadvantage with Chinese-dominated Singapore in the Malaysian Federation. Malaysia is not all that Malay. Ethnic Malays (virtually all of whom are Muslims) make up only 53 percent of "their" country's population. The Indian (10 percent) and Chinese

(35 percent) communities, descendants of earlier immigrants, are quite powerful economically. Racial strife and violence surfaced occasionally and continue to cause considerable concern in both Malaysia and Singapore. Malaysian Chinese chafe at special provisions for "bumiputras" or "native sons" (Malays) made by the Malay / Muslim-controlled government.

## Sites—Malaysia and Singapore

*Penang, Malaysia*—This island off the east coast of Malaysia is the best example of a trade-oriented, Southeast-Asian Chinese community. Much of the island's main town, Georgetown, appears to be right out of the 1930s. Human-powered tri-shaws haul passengers through dusty streets lined with dark shops selling Chinese herbal medicines or Indian spices. Stay at one of the many $5-$10-a-night Chinese hotels for atmosphere (do not expect much more than atmosphere and a bed).

*Serangoon Road, Singapore*—This section of Singapore is as close to Madras as you can get without a visa for India. Indian vegetarian restaurants (where you eat with the fingers of your right hand), sari shops, and curry vendors abound. Most of the Indians here are of south India origin and speak Tamil. The most interesting and oldest Hindu temple in the city, Sri Mariamman Temple, is in the old Chinatown section of Singapore, however. The temple's pastel tower is a maze of carved figures looking out over busy South Bridge Road.

*Geylang Serai, Singapore*—A strongly ethnic Malay area of Singapore. Go to the intersection of Geylang Road (also called Changi Road) and Joo Chiat Road. A Malay market is on the north side of Geylang Road, and Malay-owned shops and restaurants line the streets. If you are rushed, or want a good introduction to ethnic culture, see the Instant Asia Culture Show at the Singapore Cultural Theatre on Grange Road. Presentations daily at 9:45 a.m.

## Meanwhile . . . Events Outside of Asia

### Meiji Japan and British India: 1850-1900

—Italy is unified (1861)
—Suez Canal is opened (1869)

—Battle of Little Big Horn (1876)
—President James Garfield assassinated (1881)
—Cecil Rhodes founds Rhodesia (1895)
—Spanish-American War. Spain loses and cedes the Philippines, Guam, and Puerto Rico to the United States (1898)

## Republican China: 1900-1930

—Young Turks establish dictatorship in Turkey (1913)
—World War I (1914-1918)
—Russian Revolution (1917)
—League of Nations founded (1919)
—Egypt gains independence (1922)
—Wall Street Crash; Great Depression starts (1929)

## World War II: 1930-1945

—Hitler becomes Fuhrer of Germany (1934)
—Italy annexes Ethiopia (1936)
—Spanish Civil War (1936-1939)
—World War II begins in Europe (1939)
—Japanese attack Pearl Harbor (1941)
—Nazi Germany invades Soviet Union (1941)
—Allies land at Normandy (D-Day) (1944)
—United Nations formed (1945)

## Age of Nationalism: 1945-Today

—Soviets and Americans launch first satellites (1957)
—South Africa becomes a republic (1961)
—Berlin Wall is built (1961)
—Cuban missile crisis (1962)
—Civil War in Nigeria (1967-1970)
—Soviet army invades Czechoslovakia (1968)
—Americans land on moon (1969)

# III.

# Exploring Modern Asia

# 9

# Asia Today

Do not go to Asia looking for samurai, rickshaws, or sailing junks. These vestiges of old Asia are exceedingly difficult to find. Samurai exist only in Japanese comic books (manga) and movies. Rickshaws for tourists are found only at the Star Ferry in Hong Kong and on Penang Island in Malaysia. A few junks with tourists as cargo skit in and out between the huge ships in Hong Kong Harbor. Asians appreciate tourist dollars but are more concerned with the future than with the past.

Although this book is designed to help you make contact with Asia's past, you will be cheating yourself if you do not poke into the present while in Asia. Go into the grocery stores and look at what is on the shelves. Drop into one of Japan's compact but hygienic supermarkets, pick up a bottle of "Creap" coffee creamer or a chilled can of "Calpis" soda and stand in the checkout lane. Haggle with outdoor salespeople over a pair of plastic sandals in the turmoil of Seoul's Namdaemun Market. Watch TV commercials in your Shanghai hotel room. You can experience daily life as Asians do—only when you see Asia as an experience, and not as a museum, will you begin to understand what the future holds.

Today's Asia is independent, disunited, and relatively peaceful.

Japan's attempt to colonize Asia in the first half of this century and the ensuing world war dramatically changed the face of Asia. Japan went home defeated and ready for change. The European colonists returned, but in most cases only long enough to pack their bags and hand over the reins of government to the indigenous peoples.

The cold war between the superpowers (USA and USSR) was as quick to come to Asia as it was to Europe. In the last days of the war, the Soviets "liberated" northern Korea and set up a communist government in Pyongyang. The Soviets wanted in on the occupation of Japan, but the United States refused. Communist insurgencies that had been put on hold during World War II soon vied for power with noncommunist regimes, eventually winning in China, Vietnam, Laos, and Kampuchea. Communists came close to success in Malaysia, Indonesia, and the Philippines. The United States and its allies pushed communist invaders out of South Korea but failed to stop the spread of communism in Indochina. Asia, and more than one Asian country, was divided by a "Bamboo Curtain."

Only within the last decade has travel within the socialist areas of Asia opened up for tourists. Even the most accomplished capitalists are welcome in China now. Vietnam and Kampuchea have welcomed special tours (rather expensive) of Westerners in recent years. Only North Korea and Laos continue to snub their noses at tourist dollars. Obtaining a visa for North Korea remains as difficult as finding a friendly waiter in Hong Kong. For an interesting comparison of Asian-style socialism vs. capitalism, visit Peking (Beijing) and Taipei. Both cities are manifestations of Chinese culture, but the differences and similarities are instructive. There is no longer a problem getting into the People's Republic of China with the Republic of China (or vice versa) visa in your passport.

Unlike Europe, which is divided into the U.S.-led NATO and Moscow-led Warsaw Pact military organizations, no such adversarial split exists in Asia. The ASEAN (Association of Southeast Asian Nations) organization of Thailand, Singapore, Malaysia, Indonesia, the Philippines, and Brunei, is primarily a political and economic club rather than a defense organization. The communists are even less united—the Soviet Union and Vietnam are uneasy partners in opposition to China (which has aided anti-Soviet forces in Afghanistan and anti-Vietnamese forces in Kampuchea). North Korea keeps both the Soviets and the Chinese at arm's length and has to look as far as Africa and Cuba to find friends.

Trade frictions have replaced hot and cold wars as the topic of conversation in Asian capitals. The tension between capitalist East and West is palpable in the streets. Irrespective of the fairness or unfairness of the situation, U.S. demands for an opening-up of Asia's protected markets has done more to foster anti-Americanism in the streets of Asia than has any number of years of subjection to sometimes insensitive American tourists (America seems to get the blame for misconduct on the part of any Western visitor).

In the eyes of many Asians, world power is returning to Asia after an absence of thousands of years. A popular theory in places like Tokyo, Seoul, and Peking is that civilization and power arose in Asia and traveled west to Greece, Rome, London, and across the Atlantic to Washington, D.C. The same theory holds that the center of power is now somewhere out over the Pacific and headed back home to roost.

To the proponents of this theory it may seem ill-timed to point out the continuing Americanization of popular culture in Asia. Shakey's Pizza Parlors and Dunkin' Donut shops dot Japan. The world's largest Kentucky Fried Chicken franchise (three-stories high) is within a biscuit-toss of Mao's Mausoleum in Peking's Tiananmen Square. Neil Diamond's song, "They're All Coming to America," blares over bus speakers in Taiwan.

Expatriate Americans teach English language classes in community centers and corporate basements every weekday night throughout Asia. The increasing popularity of the English language makes it easier for English-speaking travelers, but the results are not always comprehensible. A Japanese youth wears a jacket emblazoned in English, "Outdoor Life For Youth—We go on an exhibition with a friend and vomit up everywhere we go—mountains, rivers, roads, and islands."

We are no more free of history than were the traveling Chinese monk/scholars, and we are no less adventurers than Marco Polo because we arrive by jet. History is happening now in Asia.

# 10

# Following in the Buddha's Footsteps

It is not always convenient to follow off-the-beaten-track historical routes, but it can be meaningful and certainly more interesting than taking crowded package tours that more often than not end up at the guide's uncle's souvenir shop. If you are in the neighborhood of Bihar State in northeastern India, consider retracing the steps of Siddhartha Gautama (see "Buddhism"—Ancient Asia) on his journey to becoming the Buddha. Try to go outside the rainy season of mid-June to September, but remember to book hotels ahead of time because there is a shortage of the tourist-class hotels.

## The Birth—A Pillar Marks the Spot

The search for the Buddha begins in Nepal at the village of Lumbini— only six miles north of the Indian border. It was in a grove of sal trees here that Queen Mayadevi gave birth to Gautama Siddhartha about 563 B.C. The parents may be forgiven for thinking that their son was special—it is said that Gautama's mom gave birth standing up and that the little fellow immediately stood up and walked around. His first words were "I am the foremost of the world." You can see the pillar

raised by King Asoka here, but the impact of the ancient monument is diminished by an ugly wrought-iron fence that keeps the curious at bay. To get to Lumbini, take a bus from nearby Bhairawa on the Nepal-India border.

## Enlightenment under the Bodhi Tree

The next stop is at a pipal tree near Gaya, India. A red sandstone slab marks the spot where, after years of meditation, the Buddha attained enlightenment or "bodhi." The tree and its descendants have been called bodhi trees since. The original tree has died and been replaced many times, as have the temples placed here since Asoka's time to venerate this cradle of Buddhism. The replacement saplings came from a bodhi tree in Anuradhapura, Sri Lanka, where saplings from the original bodhi tree were transplanted two thousand years ago by Asoka's son. About all that remains of the original second-century B.C. Mahabodhi temple are parts of the stone railing around the rebuilt temple and in the nearby museum. Many of the temple's sculptures were damaged by twelfth-century Muslim invaders. The devoutly Buddhist Burmans quickly repaired the temple. Hindus took over the site in the seventeenth century, not long after they decided to make the Buddha

one of the reincarnations of the god Vishnu. In a spirit of religious tolerance, a joint Hindu-Buddhist committee looks after the temple's remains.

From Gaya, go about 200 kilometers west to Varanasi (called Benares by the British) and Sarnath, the centers of the Hindu and Buddhist universes. Hindu Varanasi and Buddhist Sarnath have acted as twin stars wrapped in each other's gravitational pull—Varanasi burning on like a red giant next to the burned-out Sarnath.

Varanasi is the holiest Hindu city (and one of the oldest living cities) in the world; it would be a shame to miss it. Devotees of sitar music will like to know that this is Ravi Shankar's hometown. The waters of the Ganga River wash away sin, so it is de rigueur for Hindus to come to the 2,000 temples lining the banks of the river at least once a lifetime. Walking the streets of this city that has thrived since the days of Babylon, you would think that all Hindus had decided to visit on the same day. It is crowded—but then so is India. The Buddha must have found it too crowded as well; he walked on another ten kilometers to a deer park at Sarnath.

## The Sermon in Deer Park

Here, in July 528 B.C., the Buddha gave his first sermon after his enlightenment under the bodhi tree. This event took place in the Deer Park and is known as the "Setting in Motion of the Wheel of Righteousness." Thus, the wheel, a common image in Buddhist art, represents the teachings of the Buddha. Once set in motion, the wheel continues to roll of its own accord.

About two and a half centuries later, Asoka built the great stupas and

one of his many pillars on this holy ground. Muslim invaders, intolerant of other religions, completely destroyed Sarnath. Because Buddhism had fallen into decline after the third century A.D., the faithful were not around to repair the damage, and the site was left to decay until recent excavations.

The meticulous diary-keeping of traveling Chinese scholars has given us the best picture of what Sarnath looked like. The pilgrim Hsuan Tsang visited here in the seventh century A.D. and graphically described the edifices and sculpture that no longer exist.

Now go into the Sarnath Museum and find the capital (the top) of the Asokan pillar, which has been preserved here. It probably looks familiar. You have seen it all over India. This Lion Capital, with four back-to-back lions, has become the official symbol of India.

## The Final Passing Away

The last stop on the tour is to the spot where the Buddha passed away and was cremated. Kusinagara, in the Deoria District of Uttar Pradesh State, is revered by Buddhists and at one time was studded with stupas and monasteries. By the time the Chinese pilgrim Hsuan Tsang passed by, however, there was little left to remark on except for the desolation of the place. It is not known why this site was allowed to fall into ruin early on, but excavations in the past century have revealed several shrines, one of which houses a large recumbent ( a position symbolizing his death and passage into nirvana) figure of the Buddha.

## Traces of Buddhism in China

If you cannot make it to Tibet, you can experience a bit of Tibetan-style Lamaist Buddhism at the Yonghe Palace Temple in northeast Beijing.

The place was built as a palace in 1694 but became a temple in 1723 and features a fifty-nine-foot Maitreya (Buddha of the Future) Buddha carved from a sandalwood tree. Taxi or bus 116 are the best ways to get there.

In Chengdu (Sichuan Province) you can find a huge, thriving Chinese Buddhist temple called the Precious Light Monastery (Baoguangsi). It originated in the Han dynasty (second century A.D.) and sports a large collection of Buddhist art, including 500 arhat statues. A collection of Buddhist artifacts can also be seen in that city's Wen Shu Yuan Temple.

The largest Buddhist sculptures in China are at the Longmen Caves near Luoyang in Henan Province. Here, carved limestone cliffs rise on either side of the Yi River—look for most of the caves on the western cliffs. Contrast the look of inward peace on the faces of the Buddhas here to the pedantic flavor evident in the Confucian wall reliefs of the Han dynasty. The sculptors at Longmen accurately portrayed the Buddha's message of detachment.

# 11

# Hangzhou—Center of Sung Dynasty China

Hangzhou was a lot more fun 700 years ago than it is today. That is not to say that visiting the capital city of Zhejiang province today is a waste of time—I am just saying that you will not find the "pleasure grounds" near the gates of the city anymore. These state-run markets of debauchery featured brothels, satirical dramas, and assorted human oddities. Here, as nowhere else, formalities were discarded and common people and those of social standing rubbed elbows in the common pursuit of happiness. Such a place is exceedingly hard to find in today's China. When you walk the streets of Hangzhou, try to imagine it as it was in the year 1279—as the world's largest and richest city and the center of the Southern Sung dynasty. The last Sung emperor was presiding over a corrupt empire stretching from Sichuan (Szechwan) Province in the west to the plains of the lower Yangtze River in the east; and from the South China Sea to the Hwai River in the north—an area almost four times the size of France. Imagine the Mongol army of Kublai Khan as it marched south down the magnificent Imperial Way of Hangzhou (present-day Zhongshan Road) to crush the Sung Imperial Palace.

For the first time in its history, all of China fell into the hands of a foreign invader. Some say the "loose morals" of the Sung upper crust led to this disgrace; others blame factionalism within the ruling class and disaffection in the countryside. Still others point out that the Mongols were, after all, barbarians and that no one—from Mesopotamia to Europe to Korea—was able to resist their onslaught.

The Mongol success was a setback in the development of Chinese culture. Sung China was China at its most brilliant in many spheres: printing was exquisite, porcelains were skillfully manufactured and imaginative, and painting was highly developed. The Sung was also an era of great intellectual activity, social experimentation, and literary genius. Chinese cultural evolution stagnated under the Mongols, with significant progress made in only two areas, the drama and the novel.

## Art and Artists

Sung artists excelled in making narrative reliefs, some of which can be seen decorating the exterior of the Liuho Ta stone pagodas in Hangzhou today. These reliefs closely resemble the genre painting of the time, with people shown separate from each other and stiffly depicted. The ceramics of the Sung contrast sharply with those of the earlier T'ang period. Concerned more with form than with ornamentation, the Sung potters excelled in beautiful crackled celadons and black or brown enameled vases, usually with a peony motif.

The past was popular with Sung artists. Imitation antiques were coveted by Sung collectors, and bronze-casters turned out many works accentuating the traits of the earlier Shang and Chou dynasties. From the Sung on, the popularity of imitation antiques has made life difficult for art historians.

Landscape painting reached an apex during the Sung, much earlier than in Europe. The popularity of the Ch'an (Zen) meditative sect and Taoism, with its affinity for nature, contributed to a flowering of landscape painting that stressed solitude and infinity. If you look closely, you will notice that most Sung landscape scroll paintings were designed to fit end-to-end, symbolizing infinity.

## Wang An-shih—The Dirty Reformer

Even with all of the decadence and corruption of the Sung Imperial Court, the general level of education in government, monasteries, and academies was much higher than ever before. The Sung rulers improved on the competitive civil service exams that had been reinaugurated by the T'ang rulers. The Sung prime minister, Wang An-shih, rebelled against the emphasis on rote memorization of classics and promoted more practical training in astronomy, statecraft, and economics. Public schools were established in every prefecture under Wang's influence.

Wang was also known for his filth. He did not like to bathe and never washed or combed his hair. He was not alone in his unappealing habits—visiting Arab merchants were shocked to find that the Chinese did not wash themselves with water after a bowel movement but rather used "Chinese paper."

## A Walk through Hangzhou

Hangzhou is rightly called China's most scenic city. The sight of the sun rising over the West Lake is worth the trip to Hangzhou. Beautiful today, it is interesting to imagine what the lake looked like at the height of its magnificence in the thirteenth century, when Marco Polo praised it as being incomparable.

Start just before sunrise at West Lake. From one of the many arched bridges along the causeways you can watch the mist rise to reveal Chinese engaged in graceful Tai-chi Chuan exercize. Walk along the Bai Causeway to Gu Shan (Lonely Hill), an island in the lake. The Zhejiang Museum, Sun Yat-sen Garden, Pavilion of the Autumn Moon on the Calm Lake, and several tombs are on this island. Take a boat to the Three Pools Mirroring the Moon Island near the south end of the lake. This island features many pavilions joined by pleasant walks. There are four small lakes on the island.

# 12

# Beijing—A Tale of Several Cities

*The approach to Peking is tremendously impressive. Lying in an arid plain, the great, gray walls, with their magnificent towers, rise dignified and majestic. Over the tops of the walls nothing is to be seen. There are no skyscrapers within; no house is higher than the surrounding, defending ramparts.*

—*Ellen N. LaMotte,* Peking Dust, *1920*

Beijing (Peking) does not look like the old city that it is. Cruising into the city by taxi from the airport, the visitor sees broad streets lined with gargantuan, Russian-style buildings. The great walls and towers of old Beijing have been torn down by the post-1949 government to facilitate traffic flow. A few shiny glass-covered hotels and office buildings rise above the 1950ish brick boxes. The most spectacular part of the ride comes when you suddenly find yourself passing between the expansiveness of Tian'anmen (Gate of Heavenly Peace) Square and the exclusive walls of the Forbidden City.

The aura of antiquity suggested by the high, rust-red walls of the Forbidden City is quickly dissipated by the huge portrait of Mao Tse-

GATE AT PEKING.

tung (Mao Zedong) hanging over the main gate and the red and gold state logo hanging under the gate's eaves. Do not let these recent additions deceive you—this city has been around, in one form or another, for two or three thousand years.

Most of the world's great cities are situated near water and the transportation it affords. Although there are a couple of small rivers within the city limits, you will be wasting your time looking for a photogenic river in Beijing. There is not even a decent mountain in the city. There does not seem to be an obvious reason for putting one of the world's

great cities on this plain. This feeling is particularly acute if you hap-
pen to be in Beijing during the bitter and windy winter.

The Chinese also seemed to have had some second-thoughts when
it came to finding a spot for the city. The Chinese claim 3,000 years of
history for Beijing, but they have moved the metropolis and changed its
name so many times that it is hard to say just where it all started.

About 1066-771 B.C. (Western Chou) there was a town named Ji just
west of present-day Beijing. During the Warring States Period (403-221
B.C.) Ji became the capital of a kingdom called Yan. Chin Shih Huang
Ti destroyed Ji around 215 B.C., but the Chinese rebuilt it during the
Han dynasty and renamed it Yan.

Nomads out of the north continued to harass the Chinese on the
northern extension of their Yellow River-based civilization until the
T'ang dynasty (A.D. 617-907) rulers strengthened the city and renamed
it Youzhou. A northern tribe called the Kitai (Liao) invaded and
destroyed Youzhou and built their capital on top of the old one. The
Kitai renamed the city Yanjing. In turn, the Jurchen tribe defeated the
Kitai in 1125 and renamed the city of about 1 million people Zhongdu
(Central Capital). The Mongols swept out of the north in 1215 and
burned Zhongdu. This was just the beginning!

In 1271, Kublai Khan abandoned his Mongol homeland to move his
capital to Yanjing (actually a little to the northeast of the old city walls),
and renamed the city Dadu (Great Capital). His Mongol subjects
insisted on calling the city "Khanbalig" (City of the Great Khan), however, and Marco Polo referred to it as "Cambaluc" in his recollections.
In 1279 the Mongols defeated the Chinese Southern Sung dynasty, and
for the first time, Dadu (Beijing) became the political center of a united
China.

Over the years of his reign (the Yuan dynasty), Kublai built a magnificent capital city resplendent with huge city walls, palaces, broad
(twenty-four paces wide) main streets, gardens, and sculpture. To raise
the money to build the grand palaces, Kublai simply printed paper
money. No great economic genius, Kublai did not understand why
money could not be printed faster so he could build faster. Kublai died
before the inevitable inflation set in, but not before he had made Dadu
grander, larger, and better organized than any contemporary city in the
West. It was all to last less than 100 years.

In 1368, a peasant revolt overthrew the Yuan dynasty, and the leader founded the Ming dynasty, which lasted until 1644. Typically, the Ming destroyed Dadu, moved the capital elsewhere, changed their minds thirty-four years later, moved the capital back to Dadu and renamed the city Beijing (Northern Capital). This seemed to do the trick. Even when the foreign Manchus from the north took over in 1644 (after a forty-three-day takeover by a Chinese peasant leader), they kept the name and location. Instead of burning everything down, the Manchus repaired the dilapidating Ming palaces and named their dynasty the Ch'ing. Imperial China unraveled in 1911 when Sun Yatsen led a republican revolt against the Ch'ing that climaxed with the abdication of the child emperor, Pu Yi (of *The Last Emperor* movie fame). Beijing became the capital of the Republic of China, and the city survived the empire-to-republic transition without destruction.

Chiang Kaishek succeeded Sun Yatsen in 1925, and in 1928, the Generalissimo moved the capital to Nanjing (Southern Capital); Beijing was renamed Beiping (Northern Peace). The Japanese occupied Beiping from 1937 to 1945 during World War II. After the Japanese defeat, civil war raged between the Nationalists (Kuomintang) and the Communists, and by 1949, the Nationalists had retreated to the island province of Taiwan.

The Communists marched into Beiping in January 1949, changed the name back to Beijing, and proclaimed it the capital of the People's Republic of China. The Nationalists made Taipei the temporary capital of the Republic of China. The two-China situation has remained static since 1949 with both governments claiming all of China as their own. Thus, today the schizophrenic city on the North China Plain is called "Beijing" on the Chinese mainland, "Beiping" by residents of Taiwan, and "Peking" by foreigners who cannot remember which name will keep them out of trouble.

# Sites—Beijing

### Liao Dynasty

At Taoranting (Joyous Pavilion) Park in the southern part of the city near the Temple of Heaven, you can find some Liao (and Jin) dynasty pillars with Buddhist scriptures carved upon them. Look for them on the island in the middle of the lake. During Liao times (A.D. 1115-1234) this was the site of the original Temple of Mercy. The view you get from the hill on the island is the only view residents of imperial Beijing were allowed to have—all other high points in the city were occupied by the imperial family. The park was also a favorite place for despondent Beijingites to hang themselves from pine trees. Some of the old memorial archways the Communist government removed from the streets in the 1950s are on display here. Bus 102 will take you here.

## Yuan Dynasty

There is very little of Kublai Khan's Dadu left to see. The Chinese had hated being ruled by the foreign Mongols, and the Ming emperors vented their collective spleen by erasing virtually all evidence that the Mongols had ever been here. The most interesting Kublai-ism you can find today is the Drum Tower just north of Di'anmen Dajie (Gate of Earthly Peace Road). The tower was built in 1272 at the very heart of Kublai's capital and was equipped with water clocks and drums that were beaten to announce the hours. This colorful, multi-eaved wooden tower was renovated and moved a bit in 1420 by the Ming emperor.

Tianningsi Tower in the southwestern part of the city (take bus 19 or 42) was actually founded during T'ang dynasty times but it was during Kublai's time that his daughter lived here to try to atone for his wrongdoings. The tower stood outside the western walls of the Ming capital. There is also a Ming bell here that is over 400 years old.

The ancient astronomical observatory on Changan Avenue near the International Club is a reconstruction of the observatory Kublai Khan built here in 1279, and it also marks the southeast corner of the old Mongol capital. The top of the building is a good place to imagine what the old walls of the Tartar City, which converged here, looked like. During the Boxer Rebellion in 1900 (when Chinese attackers besieged the foreign diplomatic quarter), German troops took some of the astronomical instruments off to Potsdam but returned them later as a provision of the Versailles treaty. Ask "Joe" in the museum shop to show you the first Chinese compass.

To the north of the Forbidden City you can see the Dagoba Temple pagoda rising above the low buildings. Kublai Khan's court architect was from Nepal, and his pagoda is a good example of the Lamaist style of reliquary, with five parts (base, body, spire, rims, and ball-shaped top) that represent the five elements (fire, water, air, earth, and ether).

Outside the city (about twenty kilometers) in the Western Hills, visit the Temple of the Reclining Buddha to see the lacquered bronze Buddha cast during the Mongol reign. An enormous feat at the time, the statue required 250,000 kilograms of bronze and 7,000 workers to construct it. The Buddha is depicted on his deathbed, surrounded by twelve disciples. The temple was built in T'ang times but has undergone several reconstructions.

## Ming Dynasty

Much of what looks "old" in Beijing is of fifteenth-century Ming origin, although much of it was altered by the Ch'ing rulers. Li Zicheng, the peasant leader who founded the Ch'ing (Qing) dynasty, destroyed many of the Ming palaces when he drove the Ming out of the city. The great gate that dominates Tian'anmen Square today was destroyed during Li's coup and rebuilt in 1651 by the Ch'ing, who renamed it Tian'anmen (Gate of Heavenly Peace). Most of the buildings within the Forbidden City were built by Ming emperors but subsequently rebuilt by their Ch'ing successors.

Read *The Memory Palace of Matteo Ricci* by Jonathan Spence (Penguin Books, 1985) before you get to Beijing, and then go visit Ricci's tomb behind the French Church at 12 Horsetail Ditch Road (Maweigoulu). This amazing Italian Jesuit missionary / scholar / memory expert came to the Ming court in 1601 and was so well respected by the Chinese that they broke their ban on burying foreigners in China to let Ricci rest in peace here.

*Forbidden City* (Palace Museum)—This is the former palace of the Ming and Ch'ing emperors. Most of the buildings inside the walls of this 250-acre mini-city are eighteenth-century creations or renovations. The emperor rarely ventured outside these walls, and common people were not allowed inside. Opened to the public in 1927 after the emperor's expulsion, the old Forbidden City is now a remarkable open-air museum of Chinese architecture. Go early, because it takes hours to see the many ceremonial halls and imperial residences (9,000 rooms total) within these ten-meter high walls. Visitors are stopped from entering after 3:30 p.m.

*Confucius Temple*—A good place to get an overview of Beijing's history is at the Capital Museum on the grounds of the Confucius Temple in northeastern Beijing. The temple was built during Yuan times, but the museum was just opened in 1981 to house the "Brief History of Beijing" exhibition and over 1,000 artifacts unearthed in the Beijing vicinity.

# 13

# India—The Europe of Asia

Think of India as more of a continent than a nation. Roughly the same size as Western Europe, India has about 800 million inhabitants who speak over 200 different languages and dialects. The cultural differences between Kashmir in the north and Tamil Nadu in the south are as great as those between Sweden and Italy in Europe. If India's states had not been unified by the British colonialists, India could easily be a collection of different countries very much like Europe is today.

As you travel about India, get to know the states as individuals. There are interesting sites in every state, but the following list suggests a place in each state that the tuned-in traveler with a mind for history should not miss.

*Andhra Pradesh*—A part of the tenth-century Chola kingdom and later, the Princely State of Muslim Hyderabad.

Must see—The ruins of the first-century B.C. Buddhist center of Amaravati. Though a greedy nineteenth-century landowner used the 1,600-year-old marble structures for construction material, enough is left to make the trip worthwhile. Much of the ruined Great Stupa's relief carvings are in the Government Museum at Madras and the British Museum in London.

*Bihar*—Birthplace of Buddhism and Jainism as well as the seat of the Magadha and Mauryan empires. Patna was one of the world's greatest cities from 500 B.C. to A.D. 500.

Must see—The ruins of an international monastic university founded in the fifth century at Nalanda (100 kilometers from Patna). Named Sri Mahavihara Arya Bhikshu Sanghasya, the university was destroyed in 1199 by an Afghan invader.

*Bombay*—The Portuguese began development of this harbor city in 1534, but the British got the deed to the city in 1662 as part of the dowry of a Portuguese princess who married Charles II of England.

Must see—The rock-cut Hindu caves of Gharapuri Island in Bombay harbor. The eighteen-foot carving of a three-headed Shiva is the most incredible part of these caves which were carved in the seventh and eighth centuries. If you have little time, however, the caves of Ajanta (see Maharashtra below) are many times more significant.

*Calcutta*—A creation of the British colonialists who came in 1690 and left in 1949.

Must see—Victoria Memorial for Raj relics and the Kali Temple (built in 1809) for Indian architecture and the unusual.

*Delhi*—Hindu and Islamic India fused here after an Islamic Turkish invader took Delhi in A.D. 1193 and founded the Delhi Sultanate. Delhi and Agra were centers of the Moghal Empire. The British moved the capital of India back to Delhi (from Calcutta) in 1911.

Must see—Quwwatu'l (Kutb) Islam Mosque at Tomar Fortress. Finished in A.D. 1198 from pieces of destroyed Hindu temples.

*Goa*—From 1510 to 1961, this small state was a Portuguese colony. Today it is a unique blend of Iberian Catholic and Indian Hindu cultures.

Must see—Se Cathedral in Old Goa. Built in 1619, this Renaissance-style church is still one of the largest Christian churches in Asia.

*Gujarat*—A seafaring region since Greek and Roman times when Gujarati merchants traded with the Europeans. Very much influenced by Buddhist and Jain culture since Asoka's time.

Must see—The Jain sacred hill of Shatrunjaya near Palitana. The first of the 863 Jain temples was built in A.D. 960. A spectacular view of the surrounding country.

*Himachal Pradesh*—Shimla, the capital, served as the cool summer capital of British India. Rudyard Kipling's *Plain Tales from the Hills* stories were set in Shimla.

Must see—Remains of British building styles can be seen in this beautiful town, built along a mountain ridge. Autumn is the best season here.

*Karnataka*—Home of the Rashtrakuta (eighth century) and Vijayanagar (fourteenth-sixteenth century) kingdoms.

Must see—Hampi, the desolate site of the great Vijayanagar kingdom's capital. The ruins of temples and palaces are spread over about ten square miles. Destroyed by a south Indian confederacy in 1565.

*Kashmir*—Mountainous region that served as the summer retreat of Moghal emperors. Hindu rule reached its apex under King Lalitaditya in the eighth century.

Must see—Ruins of King Lalitaditya's city of Parihasapura.

*Kerala*—Also known as the Malabar Coast, this narrow state is home to people who were trading with the Phoenicians 3,000 years ago. The first state to elect a communist government in free elections.

Must see—Fort Cochin, the site of the oldest European settlement in India. The Portuguese arrived in 1500 and Albuquerque arrived in 1503 to build the fort. Vasco de Gama was here in 1502.

*Madhya Pradesh*—The cradle of Mauryan civilization and rich with more than 1,500 historical places of interest. Architecturally rich— from Asokan stupas to the erotic temple facades of the Chandellas.

Must see—The ghost city of Mandu was the capital of the Malwa kingdom. Built in the tenth century by Hindus, the isolated plateau city was taken by the Moslems in the thirteenth century.

*Madras*—The fourth-largest Indian city grew up around the British East India Company's Fort St. George.

Must see—Fort St. George, built in the 1650s, now houses the government of Tamil Nadu State. St. Mary's Church within the fort is the oldest surviving English building in India.

*Maharashtra*—Once the center of the Maratha Empire, with Pune as a capital.

Must see—The Buddhist caves of Ajanta near Aurangabad have both sculptures and rare frescoes. Buddhist monks began chipping away at the cliffs in the second century B.C. and continued for 900 years. Here you can contrast abstract Hinayana Buddhist art with the later, more realistic art of Mahayana Buddhism.

*Orissa*—The former kingdom of Kalinga, which Asoka defeated in 262 B.C. Later ruled by the Gangas, Moghals, and Marathas. Orissan temples (deuls) exhibit a distinct style.

Must see—The Jagannath Temple at Puri. Built in the twelfth century, it is the center of the cult of Jagannath, an incarnation of Vishnu. Non-Hindus cannot go inside, but the main building is sixty-five meters high, so you can see quite a lot from the outside.

*Punjab*—The cradle of Indian civilization. The Indus River civilization of 2500 includes this region. Also the center of the Sikh religion (at Amritsar).

Must see—The Sikh fortress-temple at Anandpur, near Rupar in the Himalayan foothills. Founded in the seventeenth century by the last Guru of the Sikhs.

*Rajasthan*—The ancient Indus Valley civilization included much of Rajasthan. On the traditional foreign invasion route, the area has been the battleground for Aryans, Persians, Afghans, Turks, and the British.

Must See—Jaipur, the capital of Rajastan, was built in 1728 by Maharaja Sawai Jai Singh II. Do not miss the City Palace Museum for its Islamic arts.

*Tamil Nadu*—Home of the great Chola Empire of the tenth to fourteenth centuries. Also home of Tamil culture.

Must see—Thanjavur, the capital of the Chola Empire. The 300-

foot-high Brihadeeswara Temple at Thanjavur epitomizes classic Dravidian temple architecture. The dome is a single block of granite weighing eighty tons. Do not miss the Chola murals in the covered walkways around the sanctum.

*Uttar Pradesh*—Closely associated with the beginnings of Buddhism and Jainism. The Buddha's hometown was at Piparhawa village in UP (as Uttar Pradesh is referred to). He preached his first sermon at Sarnath near Varanasi. Jaunpur was an important cultural center during the Delhi Sultanate period.

Must See—Sarnath, where the Buddha preached his first sermon. The location became a great monastic center during the reign of Asoka. Ruins and an excellent museum can be seen.

*West Bengal*—Bengal was a great seafaring nation at the time of Ptolemy and was included in his geography. Center of the Pala dynasty from the eighth to twelfth centuries.

Must see—The seventeenth-eighteenth century cultural center of Vishnupur. See the Rashmancha building for innovative architecture and the Shamroy Mandir Temple for its versions of the Hindu *Ramayana* stories.

## Calcutta—Oh, Kalikata!

Three hundred years ago, the east bank of the Hooghly River was peopleless—except for three little villages, one of which was named Kalikata. Job Charnock of the Briith East India Company—smitten with fever, no doubt—chose the spot for a company "factory" or trading center. The desolate spot was rented from the Moghal ruler Aurangzeb in 1690 and remained in British hands until India won independence in the twentieth century. For over two centuries, Calcutta (the Anglicized version of "Kalikata") was the center of British involvement in India, and it is today the best place to see what remains of the British Raj ("Raj" means "rule"). The largest city in India (8 million people), Calcutta is an open-air museum of classical British colonialism—

gardens, social clubs, and a fort very much responsible for Calcutta itself.

For William was built on the bank of the Hooghly River in 1696 to protect the English investment. The city of Calcutta simply accumulated around the fort as the locale became the center of British administration of India and the focus of British business investment in the subcontinent.

## Excuse Me, But Which Way to the Black Hole?

"The Black Hole of Calcutta" is an obscure phrase found lodged in the gray matter of many Western brains. It is neither a tar pit nor an intergalactic phenomenon, but a now-nonexistent cellar room that had but one window. Its fame derives from a gruesome incident in 1756, when 146 Englishmen and women were crammed into the room by a Bengali nawab (local ruler) who had overrun Fort William. Only thirty-three people survived their overnight stay in the Black Hole. English historians made much of the tragedy, but the only indication in Calcutta of the incident is a plaque at the General Post Office marking where the room was.

Calcutta was quickly reclaimed by the British, and the burned Fort William was rebuilt in 1773. The same year, Calcutta became the headquarters of the British administration in India and remained as the capital of India until 1911, when it was moved to Delhi because of rising nationalism in West Bengal (Calcutta is the capital of West Bengal).

The Bengalis are the artists and poets of India. Before arriving in Bengal, read some of the works of Rabindranath Tagore to get a feel for the Bengali literary tradition. Tagore (1861-1941), India's poet lauteate, won the Nobel Prize in literature in 1913. The Indian national anthem is his work. He was just one of the many contributors to a Bengali renaissance that started in the nineteenth century and fueled national pride and anticolonial feelings.

When independence finally came on August 14, 1947, the Indians did not pull down the statues of British heroes or destroy their buildings. Although crumbling (like much of Calcutta) and often renamed, the legacy of the Raj is here for the seeking.

The name changes are confusing to both visitor and resident alike.

It seems that most people know streets and buildings by their old prein-dependence names. Ask for Ho Chi Minh Street (where the U.S. Embassy is) and you will probably hear, "Oh! You mean Harrington Street?!" Try to find a map that shows both old and new names.

## Raj Relic Tour

Since Fort William is still in use you will have to see it from the outside—on the "Maidan." The Maidan (open grassy space in a city) on the east side of Fort William is a large, not-so-green park. It was designed to more or less surround the fort, so that the fort's guns could have an unob-structed field of fire. It was on the Maidan that Rabindranath Tagore made his first public speech at age fifteen.

By 1921, the British decided they did not need all that much of a field of fire and built the bulky Renaissance-style Victoria Memorial on the Maidan. Today the huge, domed building houses Victorian and Ben-gali artifacts. Statues of Queen Victoria (Empress of India) remain untouched, but the one of Lord Curzon which used to stand outside the gates has been replaced by a bronze of mystic Sri Aurobindo Ghosh. Still, this place, more than any other, is the most concrete reminder of British rule.

The sports of the Raj live on at the huge racecourse across the street from the Victoria Memorial. Races have been held here since 1819. In case you are wondering what they do with all that precious space within the racecourse oval—it has been the site of polo games since 1861.

St. Paul's Cathedral was built in 1847 and houses commemorative tablets dedicated to the British killed in the Sepoy Mutiny of 1857. It is a fine example of unremarkable Gothic architecture. Go inside to see the stained glass west window by Burne-Jones.

Also on the Maidan, at the northern end, is a 158-foot-high mon-ument to Sir David Ochterlony's victory in the Nepal wars, notable because of its mishmash of Turkish-Syrian-Egyptian motifs in honor of Ochterlony's love of things Muslim. The Indians have renamed the monument "Shaheed Minar" in honor of Indian freedom fighters.

The Botanical Gardens, laid out in 1786, is a fine example of a clas-sical English garden with rare trees, lawns, and lakes. It occupies almost 300 acres along the Hooghly River. This is where Darjeeling tea was developed.

Walk along Chowringhee Road (renamed Jawaharlal Nehru Road) near the Maidan to get a feel for the former colonial grandeur of the nineteenth century. Although many of the buildings are crumbling now, the feeling is still there. The Europeans used to live behind the facades of Chowringhee. A few old mansions remain on Park Street (formerly European Burial Road). Well-lit Dalhousie Square is a great place to walk at night for a taste of old Calcutta.

Even if you have come to Calcutta in search of the Raj era, do not miss the Kali Temple (Kalighat) south of St. Paul's Cathedral. Non-Hindus cannot go inside the temple, built in 1809, but outside you can buy one of the images of the black-skinned, blood-smeared, skull-festooned goddess Kali. Kali is one of the malevolent manifestations of Devi, Shiva's wife. Warning—daily sacrifices of animals take place in the courtyard.

Here are some other places to look for:

*St. John's Church*—Built in 1784. Job Charnock, founder of Calcutta, is buried here in an octagonal mausoleum.

*South Park Street Cemetery*—Opened in 1767, this cemetery is the resting place for many notable Europeans. A guide to the cemetery is available from the guard.

*General Post Office*—Built in 1868 on the site of the first Fort William and the infamous Black Hole of Calcutta.

*Indian Museum*—The largest in India, and superb. Calcutta has over thirty museums, but this one should be the first on your list. One of the finest collections of Gandhara period carvings is here. There is also a shocking display of brass bangles (the kind favored by Indians) found inside dead crocodiles in the zoology section. Closed on Mondays.

*Raj Bhavan*—The home of the governor of West Bengal and formerly the British Government House. Built in 1805 and modeled after Lord Curzon's home in England.

Visiting Calcutta in May or June is self-inflicted torture. The humidity and heat, combined with the crush of bodies, can make it most difficult to enjoy seeing anything. The monsoon rains begin in June and

last through September. November to February is the best time to avoid
the bad weather. By walking about early in the morning, you can avoid
much of the heat.

## Indian English—The Sounds of the Raj

An obvious remnant of the Raj is the English language spoken by many
Calcuttans, Bengalis, and Indians. You may not recognize the words
spoken to you as English, but nonetheless the English language is there
as much as it was in 1947, when the British quit India. Since the original British policy was to make good customers of the Indians, Western
education was promoted on all levels in early nineteenth-century India—and by means of the English language. Today, English is the language Indians of different linguistic groups use to communicate with
one another. There have been attempts to make Hindi the national language, but the many non-Hindi-speaking Indians have resisted.

## Indians in the Former British Colonies

You will find ethnic Indians in Malaysia, Sri Lanka, Burma, South
Africa, the Caribbean and many other areas of the former British
Empire. Many are descendants of lower-caste Indians who went
abroad as indentured servants in the late nineteenth century. By 1900
there were 2.5 million expatriate Indians in the empire. Today, ethnic
Indian minorities find themselves unwanted in many former British
colonies—from Fiji to Kenya.

### English in Calcutta—Important Dates

1696—Fort William established near Kalikata village
1756—Suraj-ud-daula captures Calcutta from British
1757—British retake Calcutta
1781—New Fort William completed
1865—first overland telegraph line connects London and Calcutta
1911—British move capital of India to Delhi (New Delhi)

# 14

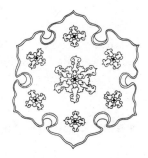

# Tibet—Medieval Asia

Tibet is best known to the outside world for its Dalai Lama and Potala Palace, symbols of its unique form of Buddhism. Much of the world has already forgotten that Tibet was an independent country until the Chinese invaded it in 1950 (or liberated it, depending on your point of view) and turned it into the Chinese province of Xizang. Isolated Tibet was its own master for most of its history, protected by the world's highest terrain and its "foreigners unwelcome" policy.

From the seventh to the ninth centuries, Tibet was ruled by kings who extended Tibetan rule over most of Central Asia and more than held their own against the Chinese. The Buddhist faith that arrived from India had a civilizing effect upon the Tibetans. Kings were replaced by a Dalai Lama, a spiritual leader in complete control of the Tibetan theocracy. When a Dalai Lama died, court experts began a search for the child who had received the reincarnated spirit of the Dalai Lama. Once found, this child became the new ruler.

Tibet was briefly conquered by the Mongols during the thirteenth century, when the Mongols ruled China. The Mongol leader Genghis Khan took a liking to the Tibetan lamas and brought some of them into his administration as advisers. During this time, Tibetan Buddhism spread to the Khan's homeland of Mongolia.

Tibet had adopted Buddhism from India between the eighth and twelfth centuries, when India was still a Buddhist realm. Tibetan Buddhism is known as Lamaism and incorporates shamanistic magic and nature spirits.

China's second dynasty of non-Chinese rulers, the Manchu or Ch'ing dynasty, again conquered Tibet in the eighteenth century, but Chinese control gradually slipped away. By 1911, when the Republican revolution began in China, Tibet was virtually independent again. Throughout the centuries, Tibet had maintained its own language, culture, religion, and currency.

From the seventh century until the last Chinese invasion in 1950, Tibet was ruled by the spiritual head of the Tibetan Buddhist religion, the Dalai Lama. Peking signed an accord with the sixteen-year-old Dalai Lama in 1951, allowing Tibet to maintain considerable autonomy. By 1958 the Chinese authorities had switched to a policy of assimilation and control. In 1959 the Dalai Lama fled the Potala Palace in the Tibetan capital of Lhasa (Place of the Gods) and established a government-in-exile in India. Ninety thousand Tibetans followed their leader across the border to India where they continue to live near him.

During the Cultural Revolution in China (late 1960s), radical Red Guards destroyed much of Tibet's tangible history, smashing Buddhist works of art and leveling ancient temples.

Many things have changed since the Chinese annexed Tibet, but the land still exudes the flavor of a medieval kingdom. In pre-1959 Tibet, the church and state were united. Most of the land was owned by religious leaders and monasteries, though the people had the right to live and work on plots assigned to them. What schooling there was, happened at the monasteries. It was as close to the Middle Ages of Europe as one could get in the first half of our century. That medieval atmosphere is best sensed today in Lhasa's lively bazaar.

Indications are that Tibetan minds remain unchanged despite Chinese assimilation efforts. Many openly yearn for the return of the Dalai Lama—and independence. Today there are over 3 million Tibetans living in Chinese-controlled territory.

# Sites—Tibet

*The Potala Palace in the capital city of Lhasa*—The Dalai Lama's thirteen-storied, 1,000-room palace was built in the seventeenth century on the site of the original seventh-century structure. Dramatic murals inside chronicle events of long-ago Tibet. Previous Dalai Lamas are buried upstairs, beneath huge Buddha statues. The decor is classical Tibetan—human skull and thighbone.

*Jokhang Temple in Lhasa*—More than thirteen hundred years old, this temple is the holiest shrine in Tibet. It is chock-full of Buddhist art treasures, the heaviest of which is the pure gold Sakyamuni Buddha image brought here from China in 652. The extent to which the Tibetans remain faithful to their religion is most evident in early morning or evening as pilgrims flock here.

## Tibetan History—Important Dates

Circa 620—Buddhism introduced to Tibet
670-692—Tibetans occupy Tarim Basin
747—Chinese expedition against Tibetans
1750—Revolt in Tibet
1950—Chinese invade Tibet
1959—The Dalai Lama flees to India

# 15

# Taiwan—Koxinga's Retreat

Taiwan does not have ancient ruins or monumental art. Tourists are often disappointed to find that the huge outdoor images of the Buddha are hollow, ferro-concrete structures housing dark museums and souvenir shops. Temples are often surrounded by hawkers selling tacky souvenirs. The purifying smoke of burning joss sticks inside the temple gives way outside to a carnival atmosphere of games of chance and tormented monkeys on leashes. What Taiwan does have for the visitor is a genuine traditional Chinese Confucian society. This alone is worth coming to see.

Taiwan is relatively new Chinese territory. It was not until the 1400s, when great numbers of Chinese from Fujian on China's southeast coast began moving to Taiwan, that the island took on a Chinese nature. Other waves of Chinese immigration swept over the island in the seventeenth century, and in 1949, when the Communists drove the Kuomintang (Nationalists) off the mainland. All Chinese on Taiwan, whether they call themselves Taiwanese or mainlanders, are immigrants or descendants of immigrants.

The original inhabitants of Taiwan are the approximately 300,000 aborigines who still live in the magnificent mountains. Tools their ancestors left behind have been radiocarbon dated at about 10,000 years. They are thought to have come from the Pacific islands, and this origin is not hard to imagine when you see their Polynesian-like features and dress and hear their music at performances staged for tourists.

The Portuguese dropped by in 1517, long enough to bequeath the name "Ilha Formosa" (or "island beautiful") to Taiwan. They did not stay, but the name Formosa has been commonly used by Westerners ever since. The Dutch East India Company came to stay in 1624 and established a fort and colonial capital at present-day Tainan in southern Taiwan. When the Dutch came there were only about 30,000 Chinese living in Taiwan.

In 1644, Manchu invaders captured Peking from the Chinese and set the Ming court retreating across China. In that year a young scholar named Zheng Cheng-gong—son of a powerful Chinese ex-pirate and his Japanese wife—entered the Imperial University at Nanking. In 1646, Zheng's father defected to the Manchu side and his mother committed suicide after being raped by Manchu soldiers. Zheng burned his scholar's robes at a Confucian temple and vowed revenge against the Manchu foreigners who had chased the last Ming emperor into Burma.

Zheng raised an army near Fuzhou on the southeast coast and soon controlled much of Fujian and Guangdong. Zheng's name was pronounced "Kuohsingyeh" in the Fujian dialect, and the Dutch, across the strait in Taiwan, began calling him "Koxinga," the name the West knows him by today. When Koxinga found his position weakened on the mainland, he retreated to the island haven of Taiwan to regroup his forces for a future counterattack against the Manchus. Meanwhile, Koxinga decided that the island was not big enough for both himself and the Dutch. Attacking the Dutch forts of Zeelandia and Providentia in Tainan harbor with 25,000 men and 800 war junks, Koxinga drove out the 2,000 Dutch after a seven-month siege.

Before Koxinga could carry out his plans to recapture the mainland for Ming China and take the Philippines away from the Spanish, he died of malaria in 1662—just a year after taking Taiwan away from the Dutch. His son and grandson ruled Taiwan until 1682, when the Manchu's Ch'ing forces managed to take Taiwan.

# Sites—Taiwan

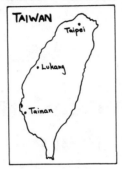

Loyalty has always been a virtue in China, even when in service to the opposition. The Ch'ing government built a temple in Tainan in memory of Koxinga's loyalty to the Ming emperor. Called the Temple of Prince Yanping (a title the court gave Koxinga in 1875), the temple and an adjacent museum contain statues of Koxinga and fifty-seven of his subordinates, many of his possessions, and a map of old Tainan harbor. Open daily from 9 a.m.-6 p.m.

Because of siltation of the harbor at Tainan, the remains of forts Zeelandia and Providentia (called "Anping Fort" and "Chihkan Tower" by the Chinese) are some distance from the sea now. What you see today are mostly recreations of these two Dutch forts of the 1650s. Nineteenth-century earthquakes and typhoons destroyed most of the original structures. A small museum of Dutch and Chinese weapons and artifacts found in the area is at Fort Providentia.

*Tainan*—The oldest city on Taiwan (and the capital until 1885) has more than reconstructed Dutch forts to offer. A bastion of Confucian conservatism and Buddhist tradition, Tainan has more than 200 temples tucked away in her side streets and alleys. Tainan was a walled city in the eighteenth and nineteenth centuries, and the great south gate (Da Nan Men) still remains in a small park about a block south of the Confucius Temple on Fuchien Road.

*Lukang*—This town on the west-central coast of Taiwan was a thriving port during the seventeenth century and preserves much of old China today. A day of walking through the narrow, twisting lanes of this old town will provide a glimpse into the heart of traditional Chinese culture. Do not overlook the very old Lungshan (Dragon Mountain) and Matsu Temples at opposite ends of Chungshan Road. Also on Chungshan Road, the Folk Arts Museum has a good selection of rare Chinese musical instruments and furniture.

# 16

# Kyoto—Smorgasbord of Japanese Culture

*"In Kioto you see the gay-colored dress of the Japanese in all its glory, for the people in Kioto have the reputation of spending most of their money on their clothes; and what is left from their clothes, they spend on the theatre."*

—*Charlotte Chaffee Gibson,* In Eastern Wonderlands, *1906*

For 1,000 years, Kyoto was the home of the Imperial court and at the vortex of Japanese culture. It was not until 1868 that the capital of Japan was moved from Kyoto (Western Capital) to the city of Edo, which was renamed Tokyo (Eastern Capital). Kyoto is such a treasure-house of Japanese history and culture that the U.S. armed forces carefully avoided bombing Kyoto (and nearby Nara) during World War II.

Walking the small lanes (what would be called back alleys in America) of Kyoto after dark is the best way to get a feel for traditional Japan. In small shops attached to homes, artisans turn out traditional pottery, lacquerware, fabrics, and porcelain in styles handed down through generations of family. The court and those who attended to it were in need of nice things, and those who could make nice things gravitated to Kyoto during the centuries the court resided here. Even after the emperor left town for Tokyo, the artisans stayed on in Kyoto.

The artisans had followed the Imperial court when it moved to Kyoto from nearby Nara in A.D. 784. The reason for the move is not known, but the new capital city was modeled after the contemporaneous Chinese capital of Chang-an. Designed on a north-south axis and surrounded by a low earth wall and moat, Kyoto was in conformity with Chinese ideas of geomancy. More than a millennium later, Kyoto still exhibits a neat checkerboard pattern of streets uncommon to Japan.

### Reading—Kyoto

*The Tale of Genji*—A classic of Japanese literature. Written by Lady Murasaki of the Imperial court in the eleventh century. Describes the decaying aristocracy and palace intrigues of the time.

## Kyoto Style

The 400-year period (A.D. 784-1185) during which the undisputed power of Japan rested with the emperor in Kyoto is known as the Heian period after the old name for Kyoto. A dramatic shift in artistic style accompanied the shift of the capital from Nara to Kyoto. Artistic Japan became more Japanese and less Chinese. Heian architecture epitomizes the Japanizing of the arts. By the middle of the Heian period, roof lines were losing their Chinese curves and adopting the straighter lines appreciated by the Japanese. The wood used in the buildings began to be cut smaller. Massiveness was out—fine detail and workmanship was in. The buildings became open, peaceful spaces—dignified and simple. The refinement of the new architecture can be seen in the following buildings.

# Sites—Heian Architecture

*Gosho (Kyoto Imperial Palace)*—Last rebuilt in 1854 to match the original Heian period structures destroyed by fire. See especially the Shisenden or main palace hall, which exudes formality.

*Byodo-in Temple*—Located at Uji a few miles south of Kyoto and famous for its Phoenix Hall (Ho-odo), this temple is the best example of the slightly more complex style that caught on in Heian times when Jodo (Pure Land) Buddhism became popular.

## The Japanese Garden

Gardens developed into an art form during Heian times, and the intellectual refinement of Kyoto encouraged garden designers. Designers of the time began to use the distant scenery (called "borrowed scenery") as an integral part of their gardens—drawing the distance into the garden.

Much of the symbolism that came to be associated with garden features was of Buddhist origin. The gardens represented Buddhist paradise—footbridges represent the bridges used by souls passing over into paradise; a central island in a pond represents Mount Sumeru (Mount Meru to Indians), the central peak of the Buddhist universe.

# Sites—Japanese Gardens

*Nijo Castle*—Kobori Enshu, called the Shakespeare of Japanese gardens by some, redesigned the gardens in 1624. The use of many large boulders creates a monumental quality.

*Katsura Villa*—Another masterpiece by Enshu; the buildings and gardens blend into one harmonious, esoteric work of art. Built in 1590.

*Saihoji Temple*—Specializes in moss—more than 100 species in various shades of green and yellow. Although fire and erosion have changed its aspect since its creation in 1339, this remains the oldest Zen garden in Japan. The design is representative of the Buddhist idea of paradise.

*Ryoan-ji*—Chances are you have seen pictures of this Zen garden with its jagged rocks in the middle of a bunch of raked gravel. Completed about 1499, the stone garden is supposedly filled with Zen meaning, but it is hard to contemplate anything while being jostled along by the crowds that come to see this famous garden.

*Sento Imperial Palace*—The beautiful garden surrounding Sento was built in the early seventeenth century. Another work of Enshu.

*Shugakuin Imperial Villa*—Built in 1629 for the retired Emperor Gomizuno, the extensive gardens feature waterfalls, ponds, and walking paths.

---

## The Shoguns

Japan's shoguns were the five-star generals of their time. The title was derived from "Seii-Taishogun" or "great general for subjugating the barbarians," the "barbarians" being the hairy Ainu people who were the first inhabitants of Japan. About A.D. 1192 the shogun Yoritomo Minamoto's power eclipsed that of the emperor, and for hundreds of years these military commanders ruled feudal Japan.

The Tokugawa shogunate, founded in 1603 by Tokugawa Iyeyasu, slapped a policy of national isolation on the Japanese people. Foreigners shipwrecked on Japan's shores were held prisoner, and the Japanese themselves were forbidden to go abroad. It was not until American navy ships appeared off Tokyo Bay in 1853 and demanded a treaty that the closed doors of Japan were pried open. The shogun's capitulation to foreign pressure (he signed on the dotted line) weakened his position and brought the emperors back into power in 1867.

## Sites—The Shoguns

*Nijo Castle*—This was Tokugawa Iyeyasu's home. Built in 1606, the place reeks of grandeur. The shogun's expansive audience halls where he met with his daimyo are simple—uncluttered with distracting furniture. The metallic gold murals and screens are the works of the best artists. The wooden floors of the shogun's halls still creak as they were designed to do over 300 years ago—to warn of approaching visitors. When Emperor Meiji came to power in 1867, the castle served as the temporary seat of government from which the edict banning the shogunate was issued.

JAPANESE GENERAL OF THE OLD TIME
(*From a Native Drawing.*)

# 17

# Bangkok

## One Night in Krungthepmahanakhoornbowornrattanakosinmahintarayuthayamahadilokpopnopparatratchathaniburiromudomratchaniwetmahasathan

After the Burmese army made a mess out of Ayuthia in 1767, the Siamese moved the capital first to Dhonburi and then across the Chao Phraya River to Ban Kok (Village o' Olives) in 1782. The official name of the capital became Krungthepmahanakhoornbowornrattanakosinmahintarayuthayamahadilokpopnopparatratchathaniburiromudomratchaniwetmahasathan (Krung Thep, "City of Angels," for short), but foreigners insist on calling it Bangkok.

## Phrabat Somdetch Phra Paramendr Maha Mongkut Phra Chau Klau Chau Yu Ilud and I

The consensus today is that Anna Leonowens significantly misrepresented the behavior of Siam's (Thailand) King Mongkut in her Victorian books about court life in Bangkok. The woman whose tales would be reworked into a popular twentieth century Broadway play parlayed her stint as a teacher to the king's children into a profitable "expose" by saucing up her writing with tales of the king's proclivity to toss errant wives into subterranean dungeons. When her books became the basis for the movie The *King and I* (starring Yul Brynner), most of the malicious lies were omitted, but the account of this important man was further fictionalized. Anna and Broadway have led us so far astray that today many Westerners do not know that the king of *The King and I* fame was a real man known to his devoted subjects as "Phrabat Somdetch Phra Paramendr Maha Mongkut Phra Chau Klau Chau Yu Ilud" (King Mongkut).

The real Mongkut, a man bearing absolutely no resemblance to Yul Brynner, took over the throne in 1851 after twenty-seven years of monkhood. Less than handsome, his haggard face was blessed with a Mick Jagger-ish mouth that drooped at one end due to paralysis. He knew several languages—including English and Latin—could calculate eclipses with his knowledge of algebra, wrote books in English, and as an amateur archaeologist discovered a stone column bearing the earliest known writing in Thai characters.

A prolific letter writer, Mongkut enjoyed issuing royal decrees to his subjects. Every possible circumstance was foreseen and advised upon; he issued decrees detailing the methods for building chimneys, for installing burglar-resistant windows, and admonished subjects about the "inelegance of throwing dead animals into waterways." The King was a generous man—he offered to send elephants to the United States "to be turned out to run wild in some jungle suitable for them." President Lincoln graciously declined.

## George Washington, King of Siam

Mongkut, and his brother the Second King (kind of an appointed "deputy king"), had a special liking for things American. While Mongkut offered elephants to the Americans, the Second King diplomatically named his eldest son George Washington. George was to become Second King in 1868 during the reign of First King Chulalongkorn. The position of Second King was abolished at the end of George's reign and the deputy king's palace turned into the National Museum.

THE LATE FIRST KING AND QUEEN.

When Mongkut was born, only Malacca, Province Wellesley, and Penang on peninsular Southeast Asia were British possessions. By the time he took the throne, the British had fought a war with Burma and annexed part of that neighboring country, acquired the island of Singapore, and were interfering in the Malay states which were claimed by Siam. The French were active in Annam and had recently bombarded an Annamese port in retaliation for the detainment of a French missionary.

Mongkut felt that by entering into diplomatic relations, allowing commerce with the Europeans and Americans, and adopting many aspects of Western science, he could avoid the troubles suffered by his neighbors. Like the Japanese, he realized that the best way to keep the Europeans at bay was to make them think they were feared and to flat-

GENERAL VIEW OF BANGKOK.

ter them with emulation. Extremely concerned with his country's image abroad, Mongkut subscribed to Singapore and British newspapers and asked foreign consuls to procure for him every book written about Siam. He was known to exhibit intense displeasure with inaccurate reportage concerning his country.

Careful both to play the European competitors off each other and to treat all equally so as to give no offense, Mongkut succeeded in keeping the Europeans out of Siam and in setting the course that enabled Siam to become the only Southeast Asian nation never to suffer European control.

## Wats—Thailand's Buddhist Temples

Wat Suthat, Wat Sakhet, Wat Po—you see names like these all over Thailand and must wonder who or what a wat is. The Thai word "wat" (pronounced like "what") simply means a Buddhist religious structure— but it generally means the whole temple complex. Thailand's wats, both in use and in ruins, are the best places to see history and art. They are the center of the community and most festivals.

Every visitor to a wat needs to know the difference between a "bot" and a "vihara." The "bot" is probably the first structure you will notice,

because it is usually the biggest and most richly adorned. This is where the monks get together to pray. The "vihara" is for the lay congregation and is where you will find the Buddha images. The swooping tiered roofs are more than ornamental—this design allows for larger structures than is possible using a single roof.

The colored tiles on the roofs were a Chinese contribution to Thai architecture. In northern Thailand, the frequent use of colored bits of glass as building decoration is a Burmese contribution. Most of the outside influence on Thai architecture, though, comes from the Khmer (Cambodians). The most readily recognizable Khmerism can be seen on the front of each roof of the "bots" and "viharas." That snakelike object is a "naga." If you ever get to Angkor Wat you will see multiple-headed "nagas" everywhere. The Thai "nagas" are, like the rest of Thai architecture, lighter and more stylized than the classical Khmer forms.

At the ends of the roof ridges you will notice horn-shaped objects. The Thais call these "cho fa" or "bunches of sky," and their original purpose probably was to ward off evil.

Stupas come in two varieties in Thailand: the "chedi" and the "prang." The chedi is domelike while prangs are slender towers. The Thais adopted and adapted the chedi from Sri Lanka and the prang from the Khmers. Stupas originated as mounds over relics of the Buddha but Buddha only had so many relics to go around—not all stupas (chedis, prangs, etc.) could get a relic, so they began to take on more of a memorial and less of a sacred significance.

The long buildings of tiny cells where the temple's monks live are called "kuti." Do not worry about stumbling into someone's kuti—they are separated from the rest of the wat by walls or canals.

Places to see the best:

## Prangs

Wat Phra Keo
Wat Arun
Ayudhya

## Chedi

Wat Mahathat at Sukhothai
Nakhon Si Thammarat

## Bot

Wat Phra Keo

## Temple Etiquette (Wat to Do)

Remember that Buddhist temples, whether in use or in ruins, are sacred ground, and visitors are expected to show proper respect, especially toward all Buddha images. Observing the following guidelines will help you avoid committing offense.

1. Dress conservatively.
2. Take your shoes off to enter the bot. Do as others do.
3. Step over, not on, thresholds.
4. Remove hats when in a temple.
5. Leave your umbrella outside.
6. Do not touch or climb on a Buddha image.
7. Do not touch a monk.

## Wat to See in Bangkok

Bangkok is loaded with wats (Buddhist temples) full of religious art and artifacts. Pace yourself, though—the sheer number of wats can leave you jaded and unappreciative if you visit them all. Begin by directing your energy toward the following wats.

*Wat Phra Keo*—Striking evidence of India's influence on ancient Thailand can be seen in the murals of the Wat Phra Keo adjoining the Grand Palace in Bangkok. Some of the painted murals along the walls depict scenes from the *Ramayana*, which the Thais call the *Ramakien*. Bearing a striking resemblance to modern Thai superhero comic books, the *Ramakien* mural is peopled by gods, goddesses, supernatural beings, devils, and assorted oddities. Looking at the finely detailed murals in this wat, one can imagine the linkage theories future archaeologists are bound to develop to explain the similarity of these murals to the Thai comic books they unearth. Even the names of the characters are similar—Hanuman (leader of Pra Ram's monkey army) and the evil Totsakan who lives in the land of Lanka.

The frescoes in the temple were originally painted during the reign of King Rama III (1824-1851), but the rotting humidity of Bangkok has necessitated repeated restorations. Despite a sloppy restoration effort in 1932, you can still "read the pictures" and get an idea of what Thai houses and dress looked like in centuries past. After seeing a few wat frescoes, you will notice that Thai homeowners did not experiment much with house plans.

This temple also houses the nation's religious good-luck charm—the Emerald Buddha. It is really made out of jasper or nephrite (a kind of jade), but since close observation is not allowed, it is hard to tell. The image is well-traveled, having been carted from fifteenth-century Chiang Rai to Lampang, then to Chiang Mai, where Laotian invaders ripped it off and took it to Laos. The Thai General Chakri (later to become first king of the Chakri dynasty) brought it back to Thailand in the mid-eighteenth century.

*Wat Bowonniwet*—King Mongkut lived at the Wat Bowonniwet as a monk prior to his career change. He became the abbot of this wat and also founded a monastic sect called the Thammayuts here. Today the wat is the headquarters of this group.

*Wat Rajanadda*—Just down the street at Wat Rajanadda you can pick up a selection of Buddhist amulets and magic charms. After much searching and bargaining (always in order outside of department stores) I found a charm for rejecting oncoming bullets for a mere 100 baht, just a fraction of the cost of a hospital stay.

*National Museum*—To appreciate the rest of Thailand, start at the National Museum in Bangkok. It is within easy walking distance of the Grand Palace. The art and history of the entire country are on display in this huge museum, and English literature is available. Closed on Mondays and Fridays. To beat the crowds arrive at 9 a.m. when the doors open. The museum closes from 12 noon to 1 p.m., so do not arrive at 11:30 a.m. When I was there, informative guided tours on art and culture (in English) were offered on Tuesday mornings.

# 18

# The Festivals of Asia

A visit to a country during its national holiday will usually mean a better chance of seeing traditional folk performances, celebrations, and exhibitions of national fervor.

The following list of festivals is not comprehensive. I have listed only those festivals I feel are worth going out of the way to see for their historical or cultural value. I will have to admit that some of them are more fun than enlightening—Thailand's version of a wet T-shirt contest, the Songkron Festival, comes to mind.

Some of the holidays you would expect to be of great interest to the tourist—are not. I once spent five boring days in Singapore during Chinese New Year's. There were no firework displays (too dangerous); all shops, including the laundries, were closed for days; and all museums and tourist attractions were closed. Chinese New Year in Singapore is for Singaporeans—families stay home and watch the government TV network's variety shows or pay visits to relatives and friends. Tourists sit in hotel rooms and contemplate their dirty laundry.

## Asian National Holidays

| | |
|---|---|
| January 4 | Burma |
| January 26 | India |
| February 4 | Sri Lanka |
| February 23 | Brunei |
| March 23 | Pakistan |
| March 26 | Bangladesh |
| April 27 | Afghanistan |
| April 29 | Japan |
| June 12 | Philippines |
| August 9 | Singapore |
| August 15 | South Korea |
| August 17 | Indonesia |
| August 31 | Malaysia |
| September 16 | Papua New Guinea |
| October 1 | People's Republic of China |
| November 7, 8 | USSR |
| December 2 | Laos |
| December 5 | Thailand |
| December 28 | Nepal |

## Calendars and Religious Holidays

Buddhist, Hindu, and Moslem festivals predominate in Asia. None of these festivals follows the West's Gregorian calendar (most are based on the lunar calendar), and so their occurrence falls on a different date each year. Check with tourist offices of the countries to find out what the festival dates are for the current year.

The most important Muslim observance is Ramadan, a month-long Islamic affair during which Muslims fast from dawn to sundown. There is not much of a cultural nature for travelers to witness—it is not even easy to find restaurants open during fasting hours. Ramadan is widely observed in Pakistan, Bangladesh, India, Malaysia, Indonesia, and Brunei. Hindu festivals are generally restricted to India. Dussehra is the most widely-observed Hindu celebration, and the one of most interest to the traveler. It is a celebration of Rama's defeat of the evil king Ravana as told in the *Ramayana* epic. The frequent reenactments of the *Ramayana* during the ten days of this festival is the tourist's best chance to see this epic played out.

Buddhists from Korea to Thailand celebrate the Buddha's birthday but not always on the same day. In Hong Kong it is celebrated on the eighth day of the fourth lunar month, while in Thailand it comes on the fifteenth day of the full moon in the sixth lunar month. Hang around the temples to witness ceremonies and look for candlelit lantern processions in the evening.

## Burma

Almost all Burmese holidays are religious (Buddhist) celebrations and fall either on new or full-moon days. If you are in Burma on one of these days of the month, simply head for a Buddhist temple and you are sure to find a festival (except during Buddhist Lent in July and August).

*Festival of Lights* (Thadingyut) occurs on varying dates in September or October and is the best opportunity to watch traditional dancing and theater. In the evening, oil lamps on bamboo floats are launched upon the Irrawaddy River to symbolize Buddha's glowing path.

## Hong Kong

*Buddha's Birthday*, May or June: Images of the Buddha are taken from temples and bathed in water containing sandalwood scent and ambergris (a substance from whale intestines found floating in the sea). The faithful drink the water for good luck after it is used in the bathing ceremony. Best place to watch is at Po Lin Monastery on Lantau Island.

*Cheung Chau Festival*, April or late May: Three or four days of Taoist celebrations on the dumbbell-shaped island of Cheung Chau. The third day is the most interesting—people parade as historical characters, and children appear to float in space (concealed wires hold them up).

*Tin Hau Festival*, April or May: A very colorful Taoist festival in honor of Tin Hau, the Goddess of Fishermen. Naturally, the activities take place in and near the sea. Brightly decorated sailing junks pay visits to seaside temple to Tin Hau. Look for performances of Chinese opera and lion dances at the Tai Miao Temple at Joss House Bay.

*Dragon Boat Festival*, June: A day of boat races in the harbor commemorating the drowning suicide of Chu Yuan, a third-century B.C. poet who threw himself into a river to protest government corruption. People raced to save him in boats but were too late.

*Festival of the Hungry Ghosts*, varying dates in August: The Cantonese version of Halloween. Ghosts are released from hell on this day and are entertained by the living with performances of Cantonese opera.

*Mid-Autumn Festival*, September: A night of moon viewing on the mountaintops of Hong Kong and the New Territories. See Taiwan festivals.

# India

*Holi Festival*, February-March: A Hindu festival marking the start of spring. Celebrants throw colored water or powder on each other.

*Buddha Purnima*, May-June: A celebration of the Buddha's birth, enlightenment, and attainment of nirvana.

*Janmastami*, August-September: A wild festival in observance of Krishna's birth. Occurs nationwide, but the most interesting celebrations are in Bombay and Mathura.

*Dussehra Festival*, September-October: The largest festival of the year lasts for ten days. Rama's defeat of the demon King Ravana is celebrated with the burning of effigies.

*Diwali Festival*, October-November: Celebrates Rama's return from exile. Oil lamps light the nights of the five-day festival to help Rama find his way home.

*Govardhana Puja*, November: A day set aside for veneration of the holy cows.

*Feast of Saint Francis Xavier*, December 3: Celebrated in Goa, where the remains of Saint Francis are buried.

## Indonesia

*Lebaran*, first day of the tenth month of the Islamic calendar: Celebrations ending Ramadan, the month of fasting. Religious services and processions start at 7 a.m. in village squares and may last for two or three days.

## Japan

The Japanese place a high priority on plentiful progeny, and they are not afraid to bring that priority right out in public. Japan's fertility festivals are unique, to say the least. Do not miss the following events.

*Tsuburosashi Festival*, June 15, Sugawara-jinja Shrine at Hamochi-machi, Niigata: Watch the performance during which an actor playing a male god dances around holding a large wooden phallus, while a female god plays a musical instrument called a "sasara."

*Tagata-jinja Honen Matsuri*, March 15, at the Tagata-jinja Shrine at Komaki-shi, Aichi: This festival is most notable for the huge wooden phalluses that are paraded about over the heads of armies of bearers.

*Bon Festival*, varied dates in August: This has to be the most colorful folk festival in Japan. Every autumn, Japanese welcome the souls of their ancestors back for a day of frivolity. Mortals dance in circles around outdoor stages called "yagura." Floating candlelit lanterns are placed in rivers and the spirits are thus sent out to sea. Best seen at Miyazu-shi, Kyoto.

# Korea

*Buddha's Birthday*, early May: Candlelit lantern processions through the streets at night. Best seen in smaller villages, but if you find your-self in Seoul, try the Chogye-sa temple.

# Macau

*Our Lady of Fatima*, May 13: This Portuguese colony is largely Catholic, and the processions on this day will put you in Portugal. Pub-lic religious ceremonies also may be seen during the Our Lord of Pas-sion observances in February or March.

# Malaysia

*Hari Raya Puasa*, first day of the tenth Moslem month: The Malay-sian version of Indonesia's Lebaran. Celebrating the end of the Muslim month of fasting (Ramadan), families pay early morning visits to ceme-teries and mosques, followed by two or three days of calling on friends and relatives.

# Nepal

*Buddha Jayanti*, varying dates in May or June: Celebration of Buddha's birthday in the land of his birth is not to be missed. Colorful pilgrimages to Buddhist shrines in Bodhnath and Swayambhunath.

*Naga Panchhami,* varying dates in July or August: A day of offerings to the "nagas," the serpents found in Hindu mythology. Kathmandu is the best place to see the traditional masked dancing called "lakhe" that accompanies this festival.

# Pakistan

*Eid-ul-Azha* (Feast of Sacrifice), tenth day of Zul-Hijja (twelfth month): Commemorates the willingness of the Prophet Ibrahim (Abraham) to sacrifice his son after seeing a vision from God. Today, Muslims substitute sheep, camels, and cows as sacrifices. The killings take place over a three-day holiday in memory of Ibrahim's submission to God. The day before the Eid, the faithful from all over the world converge on Mecca in Saudi Arabia for a pilgrimage.

*Eid-i-Milad-un-Nabi,* twelfth day of Rabi-ul-Awwal (third month): A celebration of the prophet Muhammad's birthday. Crowds gather in city centers and march through the streets, chanting verses in praise of Muhammad. Mosques are decorated with colorful strips of paper painted with verses in praise of the prophet.

*Shab-i-Barat* (The Night of Record), fourteenth day of Shaban (eighth month): The Muslim equivalent of "All Souls' Day," when the dead are remembered. Try the two special foods of the day—a pudding called "halwa" and "naan" (unleavened bread). Lots of fireworks in the cities.

*Awami Mela* (People's Festival), March: A six-day festival in Lahore that provides the traveler with the best chance to see folk traditions and crafts in one place at one time. Of special interest are the cattle displays and camel acrobatics.

## Taiwan

*Dragon Boat Festival,* May or June: Boat races in Taipei's Tamsui River. Commemorates the death in 299 B.C., of poet-statesman Chu Yuan, who drowned himself to call attention to unheeded demands for government reforms. Also called Poet's Day.

*Kuanyin's Birthday,* February or March: Interesting temple ceremonies dedicated to the Goddess of Mercy. Best place to see this is at Taipei's Lungshan Temple.

*Mooncake Festival* (Mid-Autumn Festival), fifteenth day of the eighth lunar month: It is traditional for Chinese families to gather outside at night to watch the moon and eat sticky mooncakes. Mooncakes became part of the observance after plans for a fourteenth-century rebellion against the Mongol rulers of China were passed secretly inside mooncakes. Try the campus grounds of Tunghai University in Taichung.

*Teacher's Day*, September 28: The birthday of Confucius, China's greatest teacher, is celebrated in honor of this highly-respected profession. If you can get a ticket from a Taiwan travel agency and can rise early, you may catch some very intricate ceremonies at the Confucian temples around the island. Ceremonies start at 4 a.m.

*Double Tenth*, October 10: The national day celebrating the founding of the Republic of China. Dragon dances and traditional performances in front of the Presidential Palace in Taipei. Crushing crowds and spectacular fireworks in the evening.

## Thailand

*Phra Buddhabaht Fair*, January 31 and February 1: A pilgrimage to the Temple of the Holy Footprint in the town of Saraburi. Music, folkcrafts, and dramas in Saraburi.

*Flower Carnival*, February: Flowers everywhere—decorated floats and processions in Chiang Mai.

*Loi Krathong*, varying dates in November: In the evening, candles are set afloat on banana leaves in the canals as tribute to Mae Khonka, the water goddess.

*Songkran Festival*, April 13-15: Celebrates the Thai New Year with lots of water slinging. Everyone gets into the act of throwing buckets of water on passersby.

*Visakha Bucha*, full moon in May: Celebrates Buddha's birth, enlightenment, and attainment of nirvana. Festivities center around the numerous wats (temples) and include drama and dance. Candlelit processions in the evening.

# Etcetera

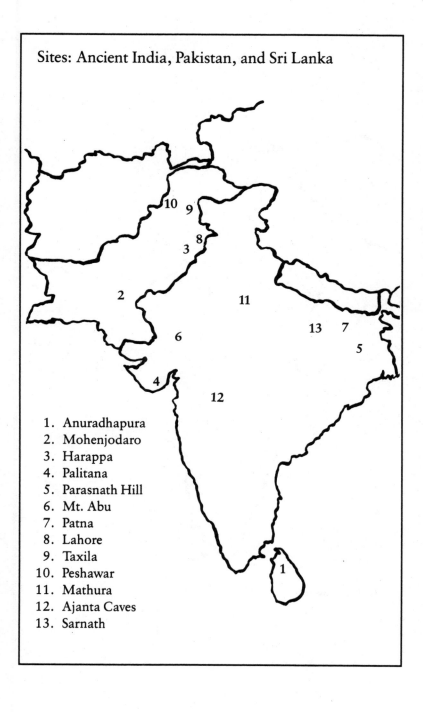

Sites: Ancient India, Pakistan, and Sri Lanka

1. Anuradhapura
2. Mohenjodaro
3. Harappa
4. Palitana
5. Parasnath Hill
6. Mt. Abu
7. Patna
8. Lahore
9. Taxila
10. Peshawar
11. Mathura
12. Ajanta Caves
13. Sarnath

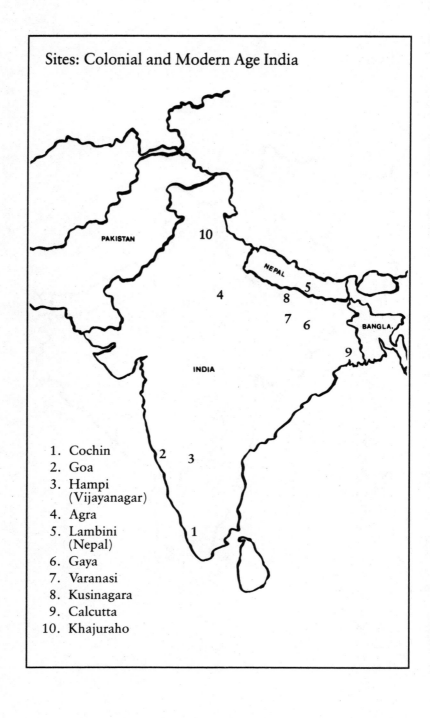

Sites: Colonial and Modern Age India

1. Cochin
2. Goa
3. Hampi
   (Vijayanagar)
4. Agra
5. Lambini
   (Nepal)
6. Gaya
7. Varanasi
8. Kusinagara
9. Calcutta
10. Khajuraho

# Sites: China

1. Anyang
2. Taipei
3. Qufu
4. Xi'an
5. Ling Canal
6. Mogao Caves
7. Maijishan Caves
8. Longmen Caves
9. Yungang Caves
10. Bingling
11. Atengxilian
12. Taihe
13. Tainan
14. Shenyang
15. Yanan
16. Hangzhou
17. Peking (Beijing)
18. Lhasa
19. Lukang

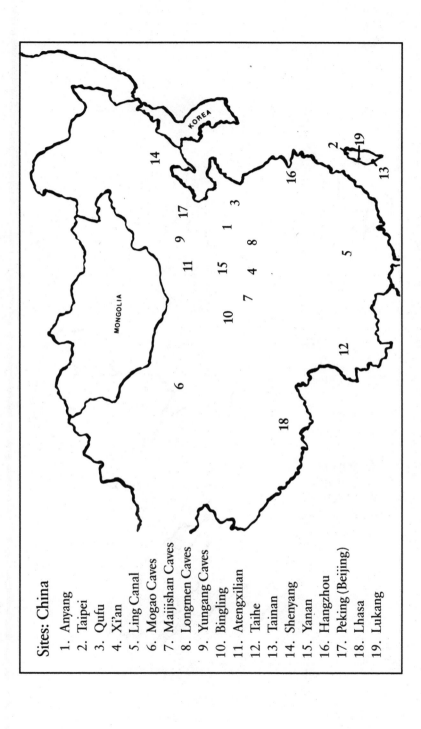

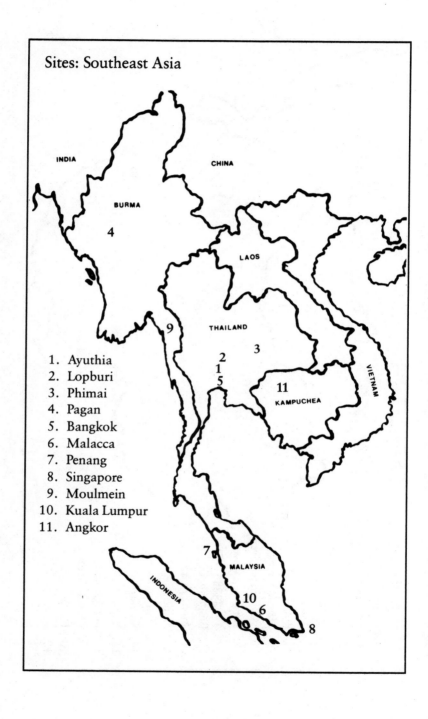

Sites: Southeast Asia

INDIA

CHINA

BURMA

4

LAOS

THAILAND

3

2
1
5

11
KAMPUCHEA

VIETNAM

1. Ayuthia
2. Lopburi
3. Phimai
4. Pagan
5. Bangkok
6. Malacca
7. Penang
8. Singapore
9. Moulmein
10. Kuala Lumpur
11. Angkor

9

7

MALAYSIA

INDONESIA

10
6

8

# Asia—The Vital Statistics

|  | Capital | Size (sq. miles) | Population (millions) |
|---|---|---|---|
| Afghanistan | Kabul | 250,000 | 14.2 |
| Bangladesh | Dhaka | 55,126 | 107.1 |
| Bhutan | Thimpu | 16,000 | 1.5 |
| Brunei | Brunei | 2,226 | .2 |
| Burma | Rangoon | 262,000 | 38.8 |
| China (mainland) | Peking | 3,768,100 | 1,062.0 |
| Hong Kong | Victoria | 400 | 5.6 |
| India | New Delhi | 1,262,275 | 800.3 |
| Indonesia | Jakarta | 582,850 | 174.9 |
| Japan | Tokyo | 143,000 | 122.2 |
| Kampuchea | Phnom Penh | 71,000 | 6.5 |
| Korea, North | Pyongyang | 46,810 | 21.4 |
| Korea, South | Seoul | 38,450 | 42.1 |
| Laos | Vientiane | 88,780 | 3.8 |
| Macau | Macau | 6 | 0.4 |
| Malaysia | Kuala Lumpur | 127,000 | 16.1 |
| Maldives | Male | 115 | .2 |
| Mongolia | Ulan Bator | 604,095 | 2.0 |
| Nepal | Kathmandu | 54,600 | 17.8 |
| Pakistan | Islamabad | 804,152 | 104.6 |
| Papua New Guinea | Port Moresby | 178,260 | 3.6 |
| Philippines | Quezon City | 116,000 | 61.5 |
| Singapore | Singapore | 225 | 2.6 |
| Sri Lanka | Colombo | 25,330 | 16.3 |
| Taiwan | Taipei | 13,890 | 19.6 |
| Thailand | Bangkok | 198,250 | 53.6 |
| Vietnam | Hanoi | 129,610 | 62.2 |

# The Nations of Asia—In a Nutshell

### Afghanistan

Afghanistan took shape as a state in 1747 under Ahmed Shah Durrani. In the twentieth century, coups have been the method of changing the government. In 1973 the monarchy was abolished and the nation became a republic. Three years later, a communist coup installed a Soviet-backed regime. In 1989 Soviet troops withdrew from Afghanistan after failing to defeat the Afghan independence fighters.

## Bangladesh

When the British quit the Indian subcontinent, it was divided into a largely Hindu India and a two-part, Muslim Pakistan. West and East Pakistan, although a single nation, where separated by 900 miles of Indian territory. East Pakistan was neglected by the West Pakistan-dominated government, and a move for autonomy for the East ended with the Pakistan army taking control of East Pakistan in 1971. A rebellion in East Pakistan brought the Indian military into the war that same year, and East Pakistan gained its independence from West Pakistan. The new nation was called Bangladesh.

## Bhutan

This is a small kingdom wedged between India and China. The Bhutanese people are thought to have come from neighboring Tibet around the ninth century. A dual government evolved, with a Buddhist lama controlling spiritual matters and an appointed leader controlling secular affairs. Since 1907 the country has been ruled by a hereditary maharaja put in place by the British. India has controlled the foreign affairs of Bhutan since Indian independence in 1947.

## Brunei

The sultanate of Brunei became a British protectorate in 1888 and remained under British control until 1984, when the tiny, oil-rich country became an independent nation. The British had hoped Brunei would become part of the new nation of Malaysia when it was formed from British colonies in 1963, but the Bruneians wanted to keep their oil monies close to home and rejected the federation.

## Burma

The Burmans arrived from the north in the eleventh century and defeated the Mons, who had dominated lower Burma for centuries. Wars with the Mon and Thai continued until the British arrived in the early nineteenth century. Burma gradually was annexed by the British and became part of British India in 1885. The Japanese occupied Burma during World War II. After the Japanese defeat, the British came back for three years until the Union of Burma became a sovereign nation in 1948. A military-socialist coup in 1962 instituted a self-imposed isolation in which outsiders were not welcome. Since the mid-1970s the country slowly has begun to reemerge.

## Hong Kong

Hong Kong is, until 1997, a British crown colony. The British have agreed to give the small territory back to China, from which it was acquired in steps between 1842 and 1898. Since the British turned the island into a city and harbor in the 1840s, the colony has served as a center of trade between China and the West.

## Indonesia

The wave of Islam swept over most of the Indonesian archipelago in the fourteenth century, washing away the political dominance of the former Hindu and Buddhist kingdoms. Islam already had sunk its roots in the area when the Portuguese arrived in the 1500s. The Dutch soon replaced the Portuguese, and by the nineteenth century, the Dutch East Indies were unified under Dutch colonial rule. World War II saw the Japanese come and go, and the Dutch try to come back. The Indonesians insisted upon independence and gained it in 1950.

## Kampuchea (Cambodia)

Formerly Cambodia, Kampuchea is the nation of the Khmer descendants of Angkor. The French established a protectorate over Cambodia in 1864 which lasted until the Japanese drove the French out in World War II. Upon Japanese defeat, the French returned but granted independence in 1953. Communist rebels captured the capital of Phnom Penh in 1975 and were in turn defeated by invading Vietnamese communist forces in 1978. The Vietnamese set up a government in Phnom Penh but much of the world recognizes a government-in-exile headed by former Prince Sihanouk.

## North Korea and South Korea

Korea remained the "hermit kingdom," paying tribute only to China, until forcibly opened up to the world by Japan in 1876. The Western nations followed suit with bilateral treaties, but by 1910 the Japanese had made Korea a colonial possession. Upon Japanese surrender at the end of World War II, the Soviets occupied northern Korea and the United States the southern part of the peninsula. Free elections to unite the country were not held, and rival governments were set up in Pyongyang (Democratic People's Republic of Korea) and Seoul (Republic of Korea). In 1950 communist North Korea invaded South Korea and came very close to overrunning the entire country before United Nations troops (mostly Americans) established a perimeter around Pusan in southeast Korea. U.N. troops pushed the communist North Koreans back and came close to taking all of North Korea, until the Communist Chinese entered the war and forced U.N. troops back south to a stalemate in 1953 near the original North-South demarcation line.

Since its founding in 1948, North Korea has been ruled by Kim Il Sung. One of the most closed societies in the world, North Korea does not welcome tourism. South Korea has experienced several military coups since its founding in 1948. The first voluntary transfer of power took place in 1988 when Chun Doo Hwan handed over the presidency to Roo Tae Woo, the winner of a bitterly contested election in December 1987. South Korea does welcome tourists.

## Laos

Laos was first united in 1353 as the Kingdom of Lan Xang, but for most of its existence has been controlled by its Thai and Vietnamese neighbors. In the 1890s Laos became part of French Indochina until 1953, when it gained independence. Rightists and leftists struggled for control until Laos fell in 1975 to the communist Pathet Lao, who established the People's Democratic Republic of Laos. Today Vietnam has troops stationed in Laos and excercises considerable political influence in the country.

## Macau

Macau was settled by the Portuguese in 1557 and used as a center for trade with the Chinese, from whom the Portuguese rented the land. In 1849 Portugal declared the settlement independent of China. Portugal tried to give Macau back to China more than once since 1967, but China refused until an agreement was reached in 1984 for the return of Macau to China in 1999. Until then, Macau will remain what Lisbon calls a "Chinese territory under Portuguese administration."

## Malaysia

The British drove the Dutch (who had booted out the Portuguese) out of the Malay states in the late eighteenth century. Within a hundred years Malaya was a British possession. In 1957 Malaya became independent and in 1963 united with British North Borneo (Sabah) and Sarawak to form the nation of Malaysia. The country is a constitutional monarchy—the weak king coming from the ranks of hereditary sultans. Islam is the official religion of Malaysia, and it is illegal to try to convert Muslims to other faiths.

## Maldives

This group of islands (and former British protectorate) off the coast of India became an independent nation in 1965. Originally Buddhists of Indo-Aryan origin, the Maldivians were told to convert to Islam by their king in A.D. 1153. Today it is virtually impossible to find a non-Muslim Maldivian.

## Mongolia

When the Chinese Empire fell to the republicans in 1911, the Mongols saw their chance (with Russian help) and declared independence. After the Bolshevik Revolution, the Russians helped a revolutionary Mongol government take power and proclaim the world's second communist state in 1924. Although the People's Republic of Mongolia owes its political existence to its role as buffer between the Soviet Union and

China, the Soviets have maintained considerable influence in Mongolia to this day.

## Nepal

The Himalayan kingdom of Nepal was hammered together by conquest in the eighteenth century. Led by the fierce king Prithvi Narayan, the small Gurkha principality extended its control over vast areas of the Himalayas and prohibited European entry. A war with the British colonialists in India in the early nineteenth century left Nepal stripped of much of its territory. Today power is shared between the monarchy and Nepal's unicameral legislature—the Panchayat.

## Pakistan

Pakistan came into being on August 14, 1947, when British India was divided into predominantly Muslim Pakistan and Hindu India and granted independence. Originally Pakistan was divided into western and eastern sections on either side of Indian territory; With Indian assistance, East Pakistan seceded in 1971 and became Bangladesh.

## Papua New Guinea

For the past century and a half, this territory has been under the control of the Germans, British, Japanese, and Australians. In 1975 Papua New Guinea became an independent nation with a parliamentary democracy.

## Philippines

The Philippines was dominated by Spain for hundreds of years, until it was handed over to the United States as part of the spoils of the Spanish-American War. Occupied by Japan from 1941 to 1945, it was granted independence from the United States on July 4, 1946.

## Singapore

Briton Sir Stamford Raffles arrived in 1819 and by 1832 turned the Malay village of Singapore into a thriving trade center. The British colony served as the center of the Straits Settlements until granted independence as part of Malaysia in 1963. Predominately Chinese, Singapore was kicked out of Malaysia in 1965 and became a republic, headed by President Lee Kuan Yew. More than twenty years later, Lee is still president.

## Sri Lanka

In the sixteenth century, the Portuguese took control of the west coast of Ceylon. They were thrown out by the Dutch, who were in turn tossed out by the British. The native Sinhalese holed up in the central island kingdom of Kandy until the British conquered all of the island in 1815. In 1948 Ceylon was granted independence, and in 1972 the nation became the Republic of Sri Lanka.

## Taiwan (Republic of China)

The Chinese lost the Sino-Japanese War in 1894, and the island of Taiwan was ceded to Japan as war spoils. After Japan's defeat in World War II, Taiwan was returned to China. The Nationalist (Kuomintang) Chinese lost the ensuing civil war with the Chinese Communists and retreated to the island province of Taiwan in 1949, moving the Republic of China government there.

## Thailand

The only Southeast Asian country to avoid colonization in modern history. Thailand still has a king (much beloved at that), but the absolute monarchy was ended in a 1932 coup. Thailand has experienced several military coups and attempted coups since the 1940s.

## Vietnam

The French were driven from their Indochina colony by the Japanese during World War II, but they returned upon the defeat of Japan in 1945. The Vietnamese fought the French until 1954, when an agreement was reached recognizing the Democratic Republic of Vietnam north of the 17th Parallel. The Americans replaced the French in southern Vietnam. South Vietnamese, Americans, South Koreans, and Australians fought the communist Viet Cong rebels and North Vietnamese until 1975, when Saigon fell to communist troops and a united Vietnam was proclaimed.

# Six of Asia's Best History Museums

If you are like most travelers, you will not be able to pop into any of the following museums on a weekend whim. To take full advantage of your time there, prepare. Before you leave home, go to your library and see if it has any illustrated books published by these museums. Most large museums, such as the National Palace Museum in Taipei, publish large-format books about their collections or special exhibits. Reading about the collections before you actually see them will greatly enhance your understanding and enjoyment. What would otherwise look like just another Chinese bronze will seem like an old friend.

In most cases, the grand national museums are in the national capitals. If, like most travelers, you enter and leave the country via the national capital, make a point to visit the museum soon after your arrival and again just before you leave. Seeing and reseeing—with an interval of field experience (touring) between—does wonders for one's understanding.

The following museums are among Asia's best.

### National Museum in Delhi, India

This is Indian art concentrate. You can explore Indian civilization in chronological order from the Harappan to the Rajput. Some areas, however, are poorly displayed. Has a good selection of publications for sale. Tuesday-Sunday, 10:00 a.m.-5:00 p.m.

## Asutosh Museum of Calcutta, India

Here is the best museum for getting in touch with the rich heritage of east India (Bengal, Orissa, and Bihar). Better displayed than the National Museum, the Asutosh has over 23,000 art objects. Pay particular attention to the Kalighat paintings. Monday-Friday 10:30 a.m.-5:00 p.m., Saturday 10:30 a.m.-1:30 p.m.

## National Museum in Bangkok, Thailand

The building that houses this magnificent collection is almost as interesting as its contents. In the nineteenth century, it was the palace of Thailand's "second (deputy) kings." Inside is the best collection of Buddhist art in Southeast Asia, as well as a good collection of Khmer and Mon art. Tuesday, Wednesday, Thursday, Saturday, Sunday, 9:00-noon and 1:00-4:00 p.m.

## National Museum in Kuala Lumpur, Malaysia

Try to see this museum before seeing much else in Malaysia—you will understand much more of the Malay culture you will be seeing. Good exhibits of Malay weapons and artifacts. Daily from 9:00 a.m.-6:00 p.m. Closed Fridays from noon to 2:45 p.m. for Muslim prayers.

## Sarawak Museum near Kuching, Malaysia

This is a good place to continue your exploration of the Malay culture of Borneo. The folk art of the tribal Malays gives an idea of what pre-Indianized Malay culture was like. For the living version, visit a Dyak community on Borneo. Monday-Thursday, 9:15 a.m.-5:15 p.m. and Saturday and Sunday 9:15 a.m.-6:00 p.m.

## National Palace Museum in Taipei, Taiwan

Here you will find the finest, and most superbly displayed, collection of Chinese art in the world. Most of the jades, scrolls, bronzes, and porcelains in this temple-style building were evacuated from the mainland to Taiwan along with the Nationalist government in 1949. This museum alone is worth stopping in Taiwan for. Allow at least a day to see it. Good selection of books available for sale. Daily, 9:00 a.m.-5:00 p.m. Sundays are crowded.

## Asia's "Top Fives" (and Sixes)—Kevin's Picks

The following is a list of Asia's top five sites in several categories. The selections will not be found engraved on a bronze plaque near the entrance to the Asian Commission on Worthy Tourist Attractions— the list is my own menu of favored selections. As with any menu, what you choose is highly subjective. I have tried to use the following criteria in making selections.

1. It has something to do with history, art, or culture.
2. It is either easy to get to or its importance overrides minor difficulties in getting there.
3. It is more enlightening, breathtaking, or significant than other sites in its category.

There is no significance to the order in which these significant sites are listed.

### Buddhist Temples

Todaiji—Nara, Japan
Horyuji—Nara, Japan
Wat Pho—Bangkok, Thailand
Pulguk-sa—Kyongju, South Korea
Miaoying—Peking, China
Borobudur—Java, Indonesia

### Big Statues of the Buddha

Daibutsu—Kamakura, Japan
Unjin Miruk—Kwanch'ok-sa, South Korea
Aukana Buddha—near Anuradhapura, Sri Lanka
Buddha of Niche 171—at Bingling, Gansu, China
Yungang—Shanxi, China

COLOSSAL COREAN IDOL—UN-JIN MIRIOK.

## Remnants of European Colonialism

Calcutta, India
The Padang—Singapore
Macao
Hong Kong
Anping Castle—Tainan, Taiwan

## Ancient Art Museums

National Palace Museum—Taipei, Taiwan
National Museum—Seoul, Korea
National Museum—Bangkok, Thailand
National Museum—New Delhi, India
Tokyo National Museum—Tokyo, Japan

## Asian Art Collections in North America

Freer Gallery of Art—Washington, D.C.
Nelson Gallery of Art—Kansas City
Cleveland Museum of Art—Cleveland
Metropolitan Museum of Art—New York City
Los Angeles County Museum of Art
Asian Art Museum of San Francisco

## Festivals

Double Tenth, October 10th—Taipei
Buddha's Birthday, May or June—Chogye-sa, Seoul
Loi Krathong, October or November—Bangkok
Songkran Festival, April—Chiang Mai, Thailand
Mid-Autumn Festival (Mooncake Festival), September or October—
    Victoria Peak, Hong Kong

## Ruins

Ayuthia, Thailand
Pagan, Burma
Hampi, Karnataka, India
Anuradhapura, Sri Lanka
Moenjodaro, Pakistan
Angkor, Kampuchea

## Best Pagodas and Stupas

Shwedagon Pagoda—Rangoon, Burma
Sanchi, India
Jetavanarama—Anuradhapura, Sri Lanka
Sakyamuni Pagoda—Shanxi, China
Horyuji Pagoda—Nara, Japan

## Modern Architecture

Daehan Life Insurance Building—Seoul
Shinjuku NS Building—Tokyo
Hong Kong and Shanghai Bank Building—Hong Kong
Akasaka Prince Hotel—Tokyo
Nakagin Capsule Tower Building—Tokyo
U.S. Embassy in Tokyo

## Palaces and Castles

Nijo Castle—Kyoto, Japan
Potala Palace—Lhasa, Tibet
Imperial Palace—Peking, China
Osaka Castle—Osaka, Japan
Kyongbok Palace—Seoul

## Favorite Works of Art

"Descent from Heaven" relief, Wat Trapang Tong Lang—Sukhothai, Thailand
Burne-Jones's portrait of Rudyard Kipling, Victoria Memorial Museum—Calcutta, India
"Yakshi from Didarganj," Patna Museum—Patna, India
"The Tien-mu Mountains in Recollection," by P'u Hsin-yu, National Palace Museum—Taipei, Taiwan
"Red Fuji," by Katsushika Hokusai, Tokyo National Museum—Tokyo

# Recommended Reading

Now that you have come to the end of the book, I feel safe in revealing that this book does not give the reader a comprehensive record of Asian history, culture, and art. You may need to consult some of the following fine books to fill in the cracks.

## General

Bowles, Gordon T. *The People of Asia*. New York: Charles Scribner's Sons, 1977.

Cary, Otis, ed. *From a Ruined Empire, Letters—Japan, China, Korea 1945-46*. Tokyo: Kodansha International Ltd., 1975.

FitzGerald, C. P. *A Concise History of East Asia*. New York: Frederick A. Praeger, Inc., 1966.

Harrison, Brian. *South-East Asia, A Short History*. New York: St. Martin's Press, 1968.

Hutt, Julia. *Understanding Far Eastern Art.* New York: E. P. Dutton, 1987.

Lach, Donald F., and Carol Flaumenhaft, eds. *Asia on the Eve of Europe's Expansion.* Englewood Cliffs, N.J.: Prentice-Hall, 1965.

Lee, Sherman E. *A History of Far Eastern Art.* New York: Harry N. Abrams, Inc. and Englewood Cliffs, N.J.: Prentice-Hall, 1973.

Myron, Robert, and Abner Sundell. *Two Faces of Asia, India and China.* Cleveland: World Publishing Co., 1967.

Reischauer, Edwin O., and John K. Fairbank. *East Asia— The Great Tradition.* Boston: Houghton Mifflin Co., 1958.

Steves, Rick and John Gottberg. *Asia Through the Back Door.* Santa Fe, N.M.: John Muir Publications, 1986.

Warburg, James P. *Western Intruders, America's Role in the Far East.* New York: Atheneum, 1967.

Welty, Paul Thomas. *The Asians, Their Heritage and Their Destiny.* Tokyo: Charles E. Tuttle Co., 1972.

## Burma

Hall, H. Fielding. *The Soul of a People.* London: Macmillan and Co., Ltd., 1913.

Stier, Wayne, and Mars Cavers. *Wide Eyes in Burma and Thailand, Finding Your Way.* Fairmont, Minn.: Meru Publishing, 1983.

Yoe, Shway. *The Burman, His Life and Notions.* New York: W. W. Norton and Co., 1963 (reprint of original 1882 edition).

## China

Chan, Albert. *The Glory and Fall of the Ming Dynasty.* Norman: University of Oklahoma Press, 1982.

Gernet, Jacques. *Daily Life in China on the Eve of the Mongol Invasion 1250-1276.* New York: Macmillan, 1962.

Goodrich, L. Carrington. *A Short History of the Chinese People.* New York: Harper Torch Books, 1943.

Huntington, Madge. *A Traveler's Guide to Chinese History.* New York: Henry Holt and Co., 1986.

Spence, Jonathan D. *The Memory Palace of Matteo Ricci.* New York: Penguin Books, 1983.

Spence, Jonathan D. *Emperor of China, Self-portrait of Kang-hsi.* New York: Vintage Books, 1975.

Zhou, Shachen. *Beijing Old and New.* Beijing: New World Press, 1984.

## India

Craven, Roy C. *Indian Art.* New York: Thames and Hudson Inc., 1985.

Insight Guides, *India.* Hong Kong: APA Productions (HK) Ltd., 1985.

Michell, George. *The Hindu Temple.* Chicago: University of Chicago Press, 1988.

Naipaul, V. S. *India, A Wounded Civilization.* New York: Vintage Books, 1976.

Nicholson, Louise. *India, A Guide for the Quality-Conscious Traveller.* Boston: Atlantic Monthly Press, 1985.

## Indonesia

Dalton, Bill. *Indonesia Handbook.* Rutland, Vt.: Moon Publications, 1978.

## Japan

Bisignani, J. D. *Japan Handbook.* Chico, Calif.: Moon Publications, 1983.

Dunn, Charles J. *Everyday Life in Traditional Japan.* Tokyo: Charles E. Tuttle Co., 1972.

Japan Travel Bureau. *Festivals of Japan.* Tokyo: Japan Travel Bureau, Inc., 1985.

Mason, R. H. P., and J. G. Caiger. *A History of Japan.* Tokyo: Charles A. Tuttle Co., 1972.

Seidensticker, Edward. *Low City, High City—Tokyo From Edo to the Earthquake.* New York: Alfred A. Knopf, 1983.

Statler, Oliver. *Japanese Inn.* New York: Random House, 1961.

## Korea

Buck, Pearl S. *The Living Reed*. New York: John Day Co., 1963.
Howe, Russell Warren. *The Koreans*. San Diego: Harcourt Brace Jovanovich, 1988.
Insight Guides. *Korea*. Englewood Cliffs, N.J.: Prentice-Hall, 1984.

## Pakistan

Santiago, Jose. *Pakistan, A Travel Survival Kit*. South Yarra, Australia: Lonely Planet Publications, 1981.

## Philippines

Bain, David Haward. *Sitting in Darkness, Americans in the Philippines*. Boston: Houghton Mifflin Co., 1984.

## Sri Lanka

Insight Guides. *Sri Lanka*. Hong Kong: APA Productions (HK) Ltd., 1984.

## Thailand

Moffat, Abbot Low. *Mongkut the King of Siam*. Ithaca: Cornell University Press, 1961.
Stier, Wayne, and Mars Cavers. *Wide Eyes in Burma and Thailand, Finding Your Way*. Fairmont, Minn.: Meru Publishing, 1983.

# Glossary

*Ainu*—The original inhabitants of Japan. Few remain of these Caucasoid people with wavy hair and "round" eyes.
*Amaterasu*—Shinto (Japanese) goddess of the Sun.
*bodhisattva*—In Buddhism, one who is capable of attaining nirvana but postpones it to stay on earth and help others.
*Bosatsu*—Japanese name for Buddha.

*Brahma*—In Hinduism, the creator of the universe.

*Brahmin*—Member of the priest class of Hinduism.

*Buddha*—Founder of Buddhism; a fifth- or sixth-century prince named Gautama Siddhartha who turned to asceticism and found enlightenment.

*Buddhism*—The religion that professes the doctrine of Gautama Buddha: that existence and suffering are inseparable but that release can be obtained through enlightenment.

*bushido*—The code of ethics followed by the samurai of Japan.

*Chola*—Ancient kingdom of south India.

*daimyo*—Japan's feudal warlords.

*dagoba*—Sinhala (Sri Lanka) word for a Buddhist stupa or pagoda.

*devala*—Hindu or Buddhist temple in Sri Lanka.

*dharma*—Buddhist or Hindu teachings; religious duty.

*donjon*—The main building of a Japanese castle.

*Dravidian*—Pertaining to the people or culture of south India.

*gaijin*—Japanese term for foreigner.

*Ganesh*—Elephant-headed Hindu god of good fortune and learning.

*Garuda*—The mythical bird ridden by Hindu god Vishnu.

*Hinayana*—The fundamentalist school of Buddhism; also known as "Theravada" or "lesser vehicle" Buddhism.

*Hinduism*—A religion native to India and characterized by beliefs in reincarnation and a supreme being of many forms.

*Indra*—Hindu god of rain and thunder.

*Islam*—A religion based upon the teachings of the prophet Muhammed.

*jataka*—A story of the Buddha's previous lives.

*jinja*—Japanese Shinto shrines.

*Kali*—Hindu goddess of death and destruction.

*Kama*—Hindu god of love.

*Kannon*—Japanese name for the Buddhist goddess of mercy.

*karma*—The concept that behavior in previous incarnations dictates one's level or form of incarnation in subsequent lives.

*Krishna*—Eighth incarnation of the Hindu god Vishnu.

*Lakshmi*—Hindu goddess of wealth; Vishnu's significant other.

*Mahayana*—Branch of Buddhism known as the "large vehicle."

*Maitreya*—The Buddha of the future.

*Majapahit*—Empire centered on Java from thirteenth to sixteenth centuries.

*mesjid*—An Islamic mosque.

*monsoon*—Arabic word for "season"; rainy season.

*mudra*—The symbolic positioning of the hands and legs of a Buddha image.

*naga*—A mythical Hindu serpent symbolic of power.

*nawab*—Indian local ruler.

*nirvana*—Buddhist concept of the release from the cycle of birth and rebirth; achievement of enlightenment.

*Raj*—Indian word for rule but usually applied to British colonial rule of India.

*raja*—Indian ruler.

*Rama*—Hero of the Hindu epic *Ramayana*.

*Ramadan*—The Muslim month of fasting from sunrise to sunset.

*ronin*—Samurai who have lost their master or lord.

*samurai*—The warrior class of feudal Japan who served warlords.

*Sanskrit*—Ancient Indian language.

*sepoy*—A native Indian soldier serving under British command.

*Shinto*—Indigenous religion of Japan. Basic tenets are ancestor worship and belief that living and inanimate objects have souls.

*Shiva*—Hindu god of destruction and creation.

*shogun*—Supreme military commander of Japan in feudal times.

*Sriwijaya*—twelfth-century empire centered in Sumatra.

*stupa*—Dome-shaped burial mound of the Buddha's remains or Buddhist relics.

*Theravada*—The "small vehicle" school of Buddhism; also called "Hinayana."

*Tirthankaras*—The twenty-four prophets or great teachers of Jainism.

*torii*—The gate at the entrance to Shinto shrines.

*Vishnu*—Hindu god of preservation.

*wat*—Buddhist temple in Thailand.


# Drop Us a Line

We want to make this guide as helpful as possible to you. Your suggestions and criticisms are welcome (send to 4339 S. Braden Pl., Tulsa, Oklahoma 74135). Xie xie.

# Index

# Other Books from John Muir Publications

**22 Days Series**
These pocket-size itineraries are a refreshing departure from ordinary guidebooks. Each author has an in-depth knowledge of the region covered and offers 22 tested daily itineraries through their favorite destinations. Included are not only "must see" attractions but also little-known villages and hidden "jewels" as well as valuable general information.

**22 Days Around the World** by R. Rapoport and B. Willes (65-31-9)
**22 Days in Alaska** by Pamela Lanier (28-68-0)
**22 Days in the American Southwest** by R. Harris (28-88-5)
**22 Days in Asia** by R. Rapoport and B. Willes (65-17-3)
**22 Days in Australia** by John Gottberg (65-40-8)
**22 Days in California** by Roger Rapoport (28-93-1)
**22 Days in China** by Gaylon Duke and Zenia Victor (28-72-9)
**22 Days in Dixie** by Richard Polese (65-18-1)
**22 Days in Europe** by Rick Steves (65-05-X)
**22 Days in Florida** by Richard Harris (65-27-0)
**22 Days in France** by Rick Steves (65-07-6)
**22 Days in Germany, Austria & Switzerland** by R. Steves (65-39-4)
**22 Days in Great Britain** by Rick Steves (65-38-6)
**22 Days in Hawaii** by Arnold Schuchter (28-92-3)
**22 Days in India** by Anurag Mathur (28-87-7)
**22 Days in Japan** by David Old (28-73-7)
**22 Days in Mexico** by S. Rogers and T. Rosa (65-41-6)
**22 Days in New England** by Anne Wright (28-96-6)
**22 Days in New Zealand** by Arnold Schuchter (28-86-9)
**22 Days in Norway, Denmark & Sweden** by R. Steves (28-83-4)
**22 Days in the Pacific Northwest** by R. Harris (28-97-4)
**22 Days in Spain & Portugal** by Rick Steves (65-06-8)
**22 Days in the West Indies** by C. & S. Morreale (28-74-5)
All 22 Days titles are 128 to 152 pages and $7.95 each, except *22 Days Around the World*, which is 192 pages and $9.95.

**"Kidding Around" Travel Guides for Children**
Written for kids eight years of age and older. Generously illustrated in two colors with imaginative characters and images. An adventure to read and a treasure to keep.
**Kidding Around Atlanta**, Anne Pedersen (65-35-1) 64 pp. $9.95
**Kidding Around London**, Sarah Lovett (65-24-6) 64 pp. $9.95
**Kidding Around Los Angeles**, Judy Cash (65-34-3) 64 pp. $9.95
**Kidding Around New York City**, Sarah Lovett (65-33-5) 64 pp. $9.95
**Kidding Around San Francisco**, Rosemary Zibart (65-23-8) 64 pp. $9.95

**Kidding Around Washington, D.C.**, Anne Pedersen (65-25-4) 64 pp. $9.95

**Asia Through the Back Door**, Rick Steves and John Gottberg (28-76-1) 336 pp. $13.95

**Buddhist America: Centers, Retreats, Practices**, Don Morreale (28-94-X) 400 pp. $12.95

**Bus Touring: Charter Vacations, U.S.A.**, Stuart Warren (28-95-8) 168 pp. $9.95

**Catholic America: Self-Renewal Centers and Retreats**, Patricia Christian-Meyer (65-20-3) 325 pp. $13.95

**Preconception: Preparing for Pregnancy and Parenthood**, Brenda E. Aikey-Keller (65-44-0) 256 pp. $13.95

**Complete Guide to Bed & Breakfasts, Inns & Guesthouses**, Pamela Lanier (65-43-2) 520 pp. $14.95

**Elderhostels: The Students' Choice**, Mildred Hyman (65-28-9) 224 pp. $12.95

**Europe 101: History & Art for the Traveler**, Rick Steves and Gene Openshaw (28-78-8) 372 pp. $12.95

**Europe Through the Back Door**, Rick Steves (65-42-4) 404 pp. $14.95

**Floating Vacations: River, Lake, and Ocean Adventures**, Michael White (65-32-7) 256 pp. $17.95

**Gypsying After 40: A Guide to Adventure and Self-Discovery**, Bob Harris (28-71-0) 264 pp. $12.95

**The Heart of Jerusalem**, Arlynn Nellhaus (28-79-6) 312 pp. $12.95

**Indian America: A Traveler's Companion**, Eagle/Walking Turtle (65-29-7) 424 pp. $16.95

**Mona Winks: Self-Guided Tours of Europe's Top Museums**, Rick Steves (28-85-0) 450 pp. $14.95

**The On and Off the Road Cookbook**, Carl Franz (28-27-3) 272 pp. $8.50

**The People's Guide to Mexico**, Carl Franz (28-99-0) 608 pp. $15.95

**The People's Guide to RV Camping in Mexico**, Carl Franz with Steve Rogers (28-91-5) 256 pp. $13.95

**Ranch Vacations: The Complete Guide to Guest and Resort, Fly-Fishing, and Cross-Country Skiing Ranches**, Eugene Kilgore (65-30-0) 392 pp. $18.95

**The Shopper's Guide to Mexico**, Steve Rogers and Tina Rosa (28-90-7) 224 pp. $9.95

**Ski Tech's Guide to Equipment, Skiwear, and Accessories**, edited by Bill Tanler (65-45-9) 144 pp. $11.95

**Ski Tech's Guide to Maintenance and Repair**, edited by Bill Tanler (65-46-7) 144 pp. $11.95

**Traveler's Guide to Asian Culture**, Kevin Chambers (65-14-9) 224 pp. $13.95

**Traveler's Guide to Healing Centers and Retreats in North America**, Martine Rudee and Jonathan Blease (65-15-7) 240 pp. $11.95

**Undiscovered Islands of the Caribbean**, Burl Willes (28-80-X) 216 pp. $12.95

## Automotive Repair Manuals

Each JMP automotive manual gives clear step-by-step instructions together with illustrations that show exactly how each system in the vehicle comes apart and goes back together. They tell everything a novice or experienced mechanic needs to know to perform periodic maintenance, tune-ups, troubleshooting, and repair of the brake, fuel and emission control, electrical, cooling, clutch, transmission, driveline, steering, and suspension systems and even rebuild the engine.

**How to Keep Your VW Alive**
(65-12-2) 424 pp. $19.95
**How to Keep Your Rabbit Alive**
(28-47-8) 420 pp. $19.95
**How to Keep Your Subaru Alive**
(65-11-4) 480 pp. $19.95
**How to Keep Your Toyota Pickup Alive** (28-81-3) 392 pp. $19.95
**How to Keep Your Datsun/ Nissan Alive** (28-65-6) 544 pp. $19.95

### Other Automotive Books

**The Greaseless Guide to Car Care Confidence: Take the Terror Out of Talking to Your Mechanic**, Mary Jackson (65-19-X) 224 pp. $14.95
**Off-Road Emergency Repair & Survival**, James Ristow (65-26-2) 160 pp. $9.95
**Road & Track's Used Car Classics**, edited by Peter Bohr (28-69-9) 272 pp. $12.95

## Ordering Information

If you cannot find our books in your local bookstore, you can order directly from us. Your books will be sent to you via UPS (for U.S. destinations), and you will receive them approximately 10 days from the time that we receive your order. Include $2.75 for the first item ordered and $.50 for each additional item to cover shipping and handling costs. UPS shipments to post office boxes take longer to arrive; if possible, please give us a street address. For airmail within the U.S., enclose $4.00 per book for shipping and handling. All foreign orders will be shipped surface rate. Please enclose $3.00 for the first item and $1.00 for each additional item. Please inquire for airmail rates.

## Method of Payment

Your order may be paid by check, money order, or credit card. We cannot be responsible for cash sent through the mail. All payments must be made in U.S. dollars drawn on a U.S. bank. Canadian postal money orders in U.S. dollars are also acceptable. For VISA, MasterCard, or American Express orders, include your card number, expiration date, and your signature, or call (505)982-4078. Books ordered on American Express cards can be shipped only to the billing address of the cardholder. Sorry, no C.O.D.'s. Residents of sunny New Mexico, add 5.625% tax to the total.

Address all orders and inquiries to:
John Muir Publications
P.O. Box 613
Santa Fe, NM 87504
(505) 982-4078